CHATHAM HOUSE SPECIAL PAPER

TERRORISM AND

INTERNATIONAL

ORDER

CHATHAM HOUSE SPECIAL PAPER

TERRORISM AND INTERNATIONAL ORDER

Lawrence Freedman, Christopher Hill, Adam Roberts,
R. J. Vincent, Paul Wilkinson and Philip Windsor

The Royal Institute of International Affairs

Routledge

*First published 1986
by Routledge & Kegan Paul Ltd*

*Reprinted 1988
by Routledge
11 New Fetter Lane, London EC4P 4EE*

*Reproduced from copy supplied by
Stephen Austin and Sons Ltd and
printed in Great Britain by
Billing and Son Ltd, Worcester*

© *Royal Institute of International Affairs 1987*

ISBN 0-415-02997-X

CIP Data available

Contents

Preface

The attack by UK-based American F-111 bombers on Libya on 15 April 1986 forced all of us in the Institute to think deeply about the issues of transnational terrorism and its impact on the international community. It raised wide-ranging questions, to which there were no easy answers. It evinced disturbingly different responses in Europe and in America in a period when the transatlantic relationship was already under considerable strain.

We decided that it would be worthwhile to pull together a collection of essays as a European contribution to the debate about terrorism and international order. We have assembled a team of authors who bring to bear on the subject a variety of views and expertise. We hope that their insights, and their exploration of the many practical, theoretical and moral dimensions of a problem which lies at the border between peace and war, will help others to clarify their own thoughts. We have not sought to impose a collective view, because we believe that this would be to oversimplify and to distort the issues.

We are deeply grateful to our authors for having willingly put aside other commitments to produce their essays rapidly. Early publication of the book would not have been possible without their generous cooperation. We are indebted, too, to a number of friends and colleagues who gave advice and comments; to Helen Wallace, Research Fellow at the Institute, who organized the project; to Pauline Wickham, the Publications Manager, without whose hard work and enthusiasm this book would not have seen the light of day; to our Library staff for their research support; and not least to Marie Lathia, who quickly and accurately word-processed many drafts.

Sir James Eberle, Director

1

Introduction

R. J. VINCENT

What makes terror—fear or dread—into an 'issue' is its systematic use by political groups in the attempt to advance their objectives. The psychological element is the distinguishing one. As Raymond Aron observed, an 'action of violence is labelled "terrorist" when its psychological effects are out of proportion to its purely physical result.'[1] And Lawrence Freedman (Chapter 5 below), in his discussion of the strategy of terrorism, marks it out as working, not through the effect of brute force on soldiers, but through the fear it engenders among civilians. This fear is induced not merely by making civilians the direct targets of violence, but also by exposing them to attacks which have a random quality, so that everyone feels less safe.[2]

In the discussion of the subject in the West, two further characteristics by which we might identify terrorism are often suggested. The first is that the methods of the terrorist are 'extreme and ruthlessly destructive'.[3] The second is that terrorism is the special method of the revolutionary organization:[4] that is, the organization whose aim it is to overthrow the state. Neither of these is convincing. Ruthless destructiveness is not the prerogative of the terrorist. The general who ordered the burning of Atlanta was not a terrorist—unless we are to stretch our ordinary language to include him. And, on the second point, Paul Wilkinson has elsewhere pointed out that 'the terror of the state is often historically antecedent to revolutionary terrorism'.[5] The ruthlessness of revolutionaries is, nevertheless, something which Western governments have associated with terrorism in contemporary international politics, and it is one of our

1

purposes in this book to investigate to what extent the association is valid, while at the same time asking a deeper question about the relationship between terrorism and international order.

It may be argued that, fundamentally, terrorism is a problem not for the international order but for the various domestic orders. The reasoning here is based on the generalization of a reading of the activities of such organizations as the Palestine Liberation Organization or the IRA as, before everything else, nationalist, such that should they achieve their aims and become nation-states, all that is required from the international system is a minor shift to accommodate the new personnel. But to follow this reasoning would be to neglect the extent to which domestic disputes have spilled over into the relations of states, and, in the case of Palestine, as Philip Windsor points out (Chapter 3), to ignore the extent to which terrorism *began* as an international problem rather than becoming one. The point of interest for us in this book is that it crosses the borderland between domestic and international politics. It is a transnational activity, in that not only does it take place between states (in which case we would not need to go beyond the expression 'international terrorism'), but it also involves groups other than states, and populations within states—even if only in the passive but crucial role of audience. Our discussion of terrorism and international order is concerned primarily with the reaction of international society to this transnational challenge.

We have, of course, all been aware of the topical attention to the African National Congress as a political organization which does not eschew the use of violent methods that might fall within our definition of terrorism. And it is an organization some of whose operations are perforce transnational. But many aspects of the current debate about the ANC, as well as the interest taken in it by Western intelligence services, demonstrate that which it is one of our concerns to emphasize: namely, the way in which the present wave of concern about terrorism risks encapsulating, and thereby distorting, the analysis of political situations like the grave one in southern Africa.

There are at least four senses in which orderly international relations are challenged by transnational terrorism. First, it violently interrupts, or threatens to, the conduct of ordinary, everyday international life—from lunch at an embassy to a summit meeting. Second, when undertaken by non-state groups, it seems to undermine the rule of international society according to which states enjoy the monopoly of the legitimate use of force.[6] Third, when undertaken, or sponsored, or encouraged, by states themselves, it seems to threaten the system of reciprocal restraint which underpins their own existence. Diplomatic immunity, the sanctity of agreements, non-interference—the principles which make possible the coexistence of states with different social systems—are not merely at risk from terrorist violence; they may also be the special target of it, as when the diplomats of other states are singled out as symbols of the operation of a corrupt system. Fourth, if, besides separate terrorist groups pursuing their separate purposes, there is also coordination among the groups in some kind of 'terror-international', then the security of the system as a whole might be under threat.[7]

How seriously the challenge to international order should be taken is a question tackled by all of our authors. Their answers to it vary, and it has not been our purpose to produce a collective solution. But certain themes recur.

The first of these concerns the novelty of the terrorist threat to international order. On this question, Adam Roberts (Chapter 2), in particular, produces interesting evidence to show that terrorist acts, and the alarm that they cause, are not a new feature of international politics. It may be, however, as Brian Jenkins has suggested, that a combination of unique political circumstances with recent technological developments, allowing mass travel, instant communication and readily usable weaponry, has produced a situation in which complex social systems are more vulnerable to terrorism than in any previous period, and more attention is paid to it because of this vulnerability.[8]

A second theme is whether terrorism is increasing. Paul Wilkinson, in his first book on the subject, referred to a 'dramatic increase in the incidence of international terrorism'.[9] And the Rand Corporation finds from its research on the subject that, 'although the level of terrorist activity oscillates from year to year, the trend over the last 12 years has been unmistakably upward'.[10] In this book (Chapter 4 below), Paul Wilkinson maintains that there is general agreement that terrorism—measured in numbers of attacks, people killed and the growth of movements around the world—is on the increase. Adam Roberts is more cautious, suggesting only that particular targets may have come under increasing attack.

A third theme is that of the attention paid to terrorism. (There is, of course, the point that attention is what terrorist groups are after, and that the chief danger they face is that of being ignored.[11] From this point of view, even a Chatham House Paper on the subject might be regarded as an accomplice to terror.) Paul Wilkinson is the most concerned of our authors that more attention be paid to countering what he takes to be a mounting threat. Lawrence Freedman is less concerned. He points out that terrorism is generally a have-nots' strategy, and that reliance on it is often a sign of strategic failure—there being not strength enough to pursue more promising policies. And while Adam Roberts argues that there is considerable justification for the view of terrorism as more than just a serious nuisance, he is equally concerned about the dangers of overreaction.

Behind the question of attention, therefore, lies a fourth theme— the judgment of the significance of terrorism in contemporary international politics. When Christopher Hill observes in Chapter 6 that terrorism has become one of the great issues on which the Western powers deliberate when they meet, what does this indicate? It might show that the Western powers have recognized, as the Reagan administration would have them do, that terrorism is the new challenge to the West, following on from the communist aggression of the 1950s (Korea), and the subversive interventions of the 1960s and 1970s (Vietnam, Central America). The Reagan line is expressed in the following quotation from an address given by George Shultz on 'low-intensity warfare':

> a . . . complicated set of new and unconventional challenges to our policy. It is the scourge of terrorism world-wide; the struggle for Nicaragua between the democratic resistance and the communist regime; it is the insurgencies against the Soviet and Cuban intervention in Angola and Ethiopia; the civil war and terrorism in Lebanon; our rescue of Grenada; and the Cambodian resistance against the Vietnamese occupation. It is the heroic struggle of the Afghan people against Soviet aggression and occupation. It is a matrix of different kinds of challenges varying in scope and scale. If they have a single feature in common, it is their ambiguity: the fact that they throw us off balance, that we grope for appropriate means to respond, and that we as a society even debate sometimes over the need to respond.[12]

Terrorism as a strategy, a means to an end, is stretched in this kind of interpretation into an enemy in itself, rather than being the sort of activity which a particular enemy might or might not get up to. And so the ambiguous challenge might justify an otherwise illegitimate response.

Another interpretation of the prominence of the issue in the deliberations of the Western powers is not that they all equally concede the danger to order that it represents, but that they routinely accept it on the agenda because of the USA's preoccupation with it. According to this view, the issue of terrorism is manipulated to maintain United States hegemony against friends and enemies alike.[13]

An alternative to both these interpretations lies in the attempt to place terrorism in the political context of the various political groups that espouse it: this approach focuses, not on terrorism, but on the objectives of the terrorist. This is the function of Philip Windsor's contribution to this book, and he deals with the particular case of the Middle East as a way of pinning down the generalizations about terrorism in contemporary international politics. Is terrorism in the international environment to be interpreted chiefly as a spillover from domestic politics? In what sense is it an autonomous activity? What is state terrorism? And are state terrorists maverick states?

Our last and perhaps richest theme concerns the response to terrorism, from the detail of how to cope with particular terrorists to more general questions about how international order is best maintained. Terrorism is a subject which, it has been said, provokes overreaction.[14] But it would be unwise, as emerges in Christopher Hill's chapter, to allow foreign policy to be taken over by the kinds of solutions to the problem endorsed in the public-opinion polls.

Our discussion begins with Adam Roberts laying out the challenge that terrorism makes to international order and scrutinizing it—which he does by analysing the theses implicit in the Tokyo declaration on the subject of May 1986. It then moves to Philip Windsor's treatment of the Middle East and terrorism. Then, in the chapter that deals most tangibly with practicalities, Paul Wilkinson both plots the changing patterns of international terrorism and examines the mounting concern of the American government. Lawrence Freedman steps back from this to discuss the strategy and tactics of terrorism from the point of view both of those who perpetrate it and of those who wish to counter it. And Christopher Hill writes on the dilemmas with which terrorism confronts the foreign policies of the leading Western states—in respect both of what to do about terrorism and of what to do about other foreign policy objectives that it obstructs.

Introduction

The occasion for this book was the attack on Libya by the United States in April 1986, and these two actors play prominent roles in our story. But we have sought to say something about terrorism and international order that transcends those places and that time. Something, but not everything. This is not a textbook on terrorism, and those interested in the psychology or the technology of terror, or its medieval origins, or its political philosophy, or in a typology of terrorism, should look elsewhere.

Notes

1. Raymond Aron, *Peace and War* (London, Weidenfeld & Nicolson, 1966), p. 170.
2. See Michael Walzer, *Just and Unjust Wars* (London, Allen Lane, 1977), p. 197.
3. Paul Wilkinson, *Political Terrorism* (London, Macmillan, 1974), p. 15.
4. 'The unlawful use or threatened use of force by a revolutionary organization against individuals or property with the intention of coercing or intimidating governments or societies, often for political or ideological purposes', US Department of Defense 1983, cited in Rushworth M. Kidder, 'Unmasking Terrorism', *Christian Science Monitor Special Report*, 21–27 June 1986, p. 82.
5. Wilkinson, *op. cit.*, p. 23.
6. This is a theme of Hedley Bull, 'Civil Violence and the International System', Adelphi Paper No. 83 (London, IISS, December 1971).
7. This is an alarming theme often dealt with in an alarmist way. See, e.g., Christopher Dobson and Ronald Payne, *The Weapons of Terror* (London, Macmillan, 1979).
8. Brian Michael Jenkins, 'Testimony Before the Senate Governmental Affairs Committee Regarding Senate Bill Against Terrorism', 27 January 1978, Rand Paper No. P-6586 (Rand Corporation, Santa Monica, CA, February 1981).
9. Wilkinson, *op. cit.*, p. 122.
10. Gail Bass, *et al., Options for US Policy on Terrorism*, Rand Report R-2764-RC (Rand Corporation, Santa Monica, CA, July 1981).
11. See Hugh Thomas, 'The Show of Violence', *The Times Literary Supplement*, 18 November 1977, p. 1338.
12. George Shultz, 'Low-Intensity Warfare: The Challenge of Ambiguity', address of 15 January 1986, reprinted in *International Legal Materials*, vol. 25 (1986), no. 1, p. 204.
13. See generally Mary Kaldor and Paul Anderson (eds.), *Mad Dogs* (London, Pluto, 1986).
14. Jenkins, 'Testimony', p. 7.

2

Terrorism and international order

ADAM ROBERTS

During the 1980s terrorism has come to be seen increasingly by Western governments as a threat to international order. Their responses to this threat have varied greatly, but there are some common elements in their analysis. It is not seen merely as a regrettable series of mini-tragedies like traffic accidents, domestic murder or 'ordinary' crime. Rather, it is widely seen as a means by which some states systematically attack others; or as a phenomenon which can lead to the collapse of civil authority in a state and its vulnerability to outside intervention, as in the Lebanon; or as an impermissible technique whereby violent minorities undermine the most basic principles of democratic systems, the right of the people to freely express their views and determine the shape of government; or as a contagion which, even if started in a noble cause, quickly gets out of hand, destroying internal and international order alike.

This view, that terrorism is not merely a serious nuisance but also a threat to international order, has considerable justification. Many international crises and conflicts of the late 1970s and the 1980s followed acts which indeed deserved the label 'terrorist': for example, the seizure of US hostages in Iran in November 1979, the shooting of the Israeli ambassador to London in June 1982, the attacks on Rome and Vienna airports in December 1985, and so on.

The current state of thinking among Western governments about the problem of terrorism is best encapsulated, in a simplified form, in the declaration on terrorism issued on 6 May 1986 by the leaders of seven major industrial countries meeting in Tokyo, and most particularly in its first paragraph:

> We, the heads of state or government of seven major democracies and the representatives of the European Community, assembled here in Tokyo, strongly reaffirm our condemnation of international terrorism in all its forms, of its accomplices and of those, including governments, who sponsor or support it. We abhor the increase in the level of such terrorism since our last meeting, and in particular its blatant and cynical use as an instrument of government policy. Terrorism has no justification. It spreads only by use of contemptible means, ignoring the values of human life, freedom and dignity. It must be fought relentlessly and without compromise.

The approach to the problem of terrorism which is implicit in this paragraph of the Tokyo declaration, and is more or less explicit in some of the rest of the document, can be said to contain the following elements:

(1) 'Terrorism' and 'international terrorism' do not need to be defined: we all know what we are talking about.
(2) There has been an increase in terrorism in the year since the Bonn summit of 2–4 May 1985.
(3) 'Terrorism has no justification.' It is such a morally contemptible means of struggle that it is absolutely wrong in all circumstances.
(4) There are some governments which sponsor or support terrorism, and make 'blatant and cynical use' of it. Libya is specifically mentioned in the fourth paragraph of the Tokyo declaration as one such country.
(5) Terrorism must be fought 'relentlessly and without compromise'.

All five of these elements are open to one kind of criticism or another. They are considered in turn in this paper. To draw attention to such possible lines of criticism is not to deny the value of the Tokyo declaration, which had to be expressed in brief and forthright terms, acceptable to all the governments represented at the summit. In fact both the analyses which inform the declaration, and the courses of action flowing from it, have necessarily to be more nuanced and reflective than the declaration itself.

(1) Definitions of terrorism

Often in the political realm there is no point in worrying about definitions. The core meaning of a term is clear even if its exact frontiers are not. If—in the name of some political cause—a bomb goes off in an aircraft, a crowded hotel or a shop, or if such destruction is convincingly threatened, most people are prepared, perfectly reasonably, to call it 'terrorism'.

The history of international discussions on terrorism suggests that there are especially strong reasons for avoiding an excessive pre-occupation with definitions. There have long been genuine difficulties in getting any widespread agreement as to what constitutes terrorism. Often in such discussions a concern with defining terrorism or with explaining its causes has been the outward and visible sign of a reluctance to recognize the seriousness of the problem or to do anything at all about it.

However, even when use of the term 'terrorism' is factually justified there are dangers in attaching such a dismissive label to a bewilderingly wide variety of acts: such a label may actually inhibit understanding and lead to ill-considered policies by way of response. There are similar dangers in attaching the label to organizations. In many studies on terrorism, it seems to be assumed that organizations can be neatly categorized as 'terrorist' or otherwise. Reality is often rather messier.

The fact that very few people call themselves terrorists is of relatively minor importance. The Russian Tsar-killers of the late nineteenth century were proud of the label; and indeed they brought the modern meaning of such words as 'terrorism' and 'terrorist' into common political usage. But few others have welcomed being classified as terrorist. As Menachem Begin, who later became Prime Minister of Israel, wrote in his account of the Irgun movement in Palestine:

> Our enemies called us terrorists. People who were neither friends nor enemies, like the correspondents of the *New York Herald Tribune*, also used this Latin name, either under the influence of British propaganda or out of habit. Our friends, like the Irishman O'Reilly, preferred, as he

wrote in his letter, to 'get ahead of history' and called us by a simpler, though also a Latin, name: patriots.[1]

But whether or not people like being called 'terrorists' is not the only issue. There are two other grounds for doubt. The use of the term 'terrorist' carries the implications (a) that terror is the primary, or even the sole, mechanism on which a group relies; and (b) that it is the use of terror which distinguishes the group from its opponents.

Both these implications may be questionable in a particular situation. The Vietnam war between about 1960 and 1975 provided a striking example. In the 1960s many writers and journalists freely used the word 'terrorist' to describe a member of the Vietcong, the military arm of the National Liberation Front in South Vietnam. But such usage only begged the question as to whether terror was the primary means of control; and whether it was 'terror' itself, or some other characteristic, which distinguished the insurgent group from its rivals and opponents.[2] In Vietnam it was always clear that extensive terror was used on the side of Saigon as well as on that of its adversaries.

Likewise, in the Middle East today, the Palestinian Arabs tend to take the view that the Palestine Liberation Organization (PLO) is largely a political entity—even if it is one with terroristic and coercive wings. They also tend to argue that attacks against some civilian targets are a regrettable but necessary way of making the world aware of the historic wrongs done to the Palestinians by various governments, Western and Israeli. Rightly or wrongly, they therefore doubly resent the simple attaching of the label 'terrorist' exclusively to the PLO and not at all to its adversaries.

Governmental uses of terror

That many governments use terror systematically as an instrument of internal control is beyond dispute. The terror in France between March 1793 and July 1794 is a case in point. So is Stalin's great terror in the Soviet Union in the 1930s.[3] The relationship between such governmental uses of terror and the question of international order is complex.

First, there is the question of whether terror can provide a basis for order in human societies.[4] It would be nice to record that governmental terror always fails or tends to be counterproductive, but it is by no means always so in the short term. The Yugoslav writer Milovan Djilas has gone so far as to suggest that Stalin's great terror may actually have helped the communist system to survive.[5] On the other hand, extreme uses of terror by governments are frequently both a symptom and a guarantee of weakness on the part of those who wield the terror. The Czechoslovak mass trials of the early 1950s, and the Greek use of torture in the years 1967–75, were both examples of the use of terror by insecure regimes; and, in both cases, the issue of terror contributed to subsequent crises within the regimes.

Second, there is the question of whether internally terroristic regimes are more likely than others to act aggressively abroad, whether by open military attacks on other countries or by covert terrorist action. Despite some possible contrary examples (Stalin before World War II and France during it), there does seem some evidence to support the proposition. This may be not only because such regimes in general have relatively few inhibitions about the use of force, but also because of their tendency to drive internal opposition into foreign exile and then, having done so, to hunt opposition members down with hit squads.

The alleged governmental use of terror which has given rise to so much concern in recent years has had a special character. It has consisted of various forms of more or less clandestine governmental assistance to, and control of, non-governmental groups such as the Provisional IRA, various branches of the PLO, and so on. In this form, terrorism appears to have many of the resources of governments at its disposal, even including, in some cases, the use of diplomatic premises, while at the same time there is no one openly answerable for its actions in the way that the government of a state must answer for its openly avowed actions.

Although state-sponsored terrorism is a major preoccupation of Western governments today, there are dangers in excessive preoccupation with this aspect. It is an area in which facts are scarce and lurid theories abundant. It remains a matter for judgment what kind of support governments give to terrorist groups, what degree of control they actually have over any groups to which they have given some kind of support, and how they use such control. Moreover, in many Third World countries, from Lebanon to India, the trend in the 1980s seems to have been towards terrorist campaigns which have a life of their own and which are beyond the control of any

Terrorism and international order

state. It may be because such terrorism is increasingly recognized as a threat to order in many Third World states that there have been recent signs of at least some general international consensus on the need to tackle the problem.

International attempts at defining and outlawing terrorism

There have been many international negotiations in the past two decades in which the attempt has been made to define and outlaw terrorism. The history of these attempts, although it has by no means been entirely fruitless, is evidence of the genuine difficulties inevitably involved in any such enterprise. Non-lawyers often have exaggerated notions of what international law can say and do: often the best that can be hoped for still leaves open much room for interpretation.

The United Nations General Assembly, largely through the work of its Sixth Committee, has discussed the matter at considerable length, and with some positive result. One outcome of its work was the Declaration on Principles of International Law Concerning Friendly Relations and Co-operation Among States in Accordance with the Charter of the United Nations. This declaration, which was approved by the UN General Assembly on 24 October 1970, says in part:

> Every State has the duty to refrain from organizing or encouraging the organization of irregular forces or armed bands, including mercenaries, for incursion into the territory of another State.
> Every State has the duty to refrain from organizing, instigating, assisting or participating in acts of civil strife or terrorist acts in another State or acquiescing in organized activities within its territory directed towards the commission of such acts, when the acts referred to in the present paragraph involve a threat or use of force...

Similarly the UN Definition of Aggression, approved by the UN General Assembly on 14 December 1974, includes the following in Article 3 as one type of act which qualifies as an act of aggression:

> (g) The sending by or on behalf of a State of armed bands, groups, irregulars or mercenaries, which carry out acts of armed force against

another State of such gravity as to amount to the acts listed above, or its substantial involvement therein.[6]

However, both these documents contain a significant caveat in respect of struggles by peoples forcibly deprived of the right of self-determination. As the 1974 Definition of Aggression, Article 7, put it:

Nothing in this Definition, and in particular Article 3, could in any way prejudice the right to self-determination, freedom and independence, as derived from the Charter, of peoples forcibly deprived of that right and referred to in the Declaration on Principles of International Law concerning Friendly Relations and Co-operation among States in accordance with the Charter of the United Nations, particularly peoples under colonial and racist regimes or other forms of alien domination; nor the right of these peoples to struggle to that end and to seek and receive support, in accordance with the principles of the Charter and in conformity with the above-mentioned Declaration.

Thus, as far as the outlawing of international terrorism goes, the General Assembly has achieved little except in those cases, surely very few, which cannot be fitted into the exculpatory framework of struggle by peoples forcibly deprived of their right of self-determination. However, in the light of developments in the 1980s, especially the threat posed by terrorism to various Third World states, including India and Lebanon, there was more evidence of willingness to condemn terrorism. On 9 December 1985, the UN General Assembly adopted for the first time a condemnation of terrorism in all its forms. The General Assembly, to quote from Resolution 40/61, 'condemns as criminal all acts, methods and practices of terrorism wherever and by whomever committed'. At the same time the General Assembly did reaffirm the legitimacy of struggles for self-determination.

In addition to such generalized attempts to define and outlaw terrorism as such, the international community has also at times concentrated its attention more narrowly—and perhaps more usefully—on 'specific activities that are capable of being outlawed'. These have included the hijacking of aircraft, which is dealt with in three major conventions on civil aviation;[7] and hostage-taking, which is addressed in the 1979 International Convention Against the

Taking of Hostages. All these agreements apply the 'extradite or prosecute' rule to the crimes with which they deal.

The 1979 Convention Against the Taking of Hostages (which entered into force on 3 June 1983) deals with hostage-taking in peacetime, and refers specifically to terrorism in the preamble, which says:

> ... it is urgently necessary to develop international co-operation between states in devising and adopting effective measures for the prevention, prosecution and punishment of all acts of taking of hostages as manifestations of international terrorism ...

Another approach to international legal prohibition of terrorism has been through the laws of war. This approach relates of course specifically to conditions of more or less open hostilities. However, the enunciation of general principles as to what is, or is not, a legitimate means of struggle or a legitimate target in warfare may have implications also for how activities by terrorist groups and their adversaries, even in peacetime, are judged.

The two 1977 Protocols Additional to the 1949 Geneva Conventions have a potential bearing on terrorism in several ways. The first of these Protocols, dealing with international armed conflicts, including not only regular inter-state wars but also certain struggles by peoples fighting 'in the exercise of their right of self-determination', contains many provisions (especially in Articles 48–79) prohibiting attacks on civilian targets, etc. Yet by an odd irony, and for reasons which scarcely stand up to a careful reading of the text as a whole, the Reagan administration has called this document a 'terrorists' charter'. Along with many of its allies, the USA has refused to ratify it. The second of these 1977 Protocols, dealing with non-international armed conflicts, and also unratified by most Western powers, says in Article 13, paragraph 2:

> The civilian population as such, as well as individual civilians, shall not be the object of attack. Acts or threats of violence the primary purpose of which is to spread terror among the civilian population are prohibited.

Among the numerous reasons why many governments have been unenthusiastic about these two 1977 Protocols may be an unease about the whole principle of coping with terrorism in a laws-of-war framework. Such a framework may seem to imply a degree of moral acceptance of the right of a given group to resort to acts of violence at all. Furthermore, a laws-of-war framework, however much it may restrict the actions of terrorists so far as the choice of targets is concerned, is always likely to leave the armed forces as a legitimate target, so does not necessarily reduce the risks to US marines in Beirut or to US servicemen in a West Berlin discotheque. Thirdly, a laws-of-war framework may hamper some counterterrorist acts by states: the prohibitions on reprisals in the 1977 Geneva Protocol I, Articles 52–6, are a possible case in point.

Although there have been some achievements, it is easy to be critical of the meagre results which have flowed from the various diplomatic efforts aimed at defining and outlawing terrorism. The blame for this failure is easily laid at the door of the United Nations, or of those states which are believed to support terrorism in one form or another. However, the history of these efforts also shows that there are genuine difficulties in defining what terrorism is, and in agreeing on whether the problem should be addressed in a laws-of-war framework or otherwise. There are problems not just between states, but also to some extent within them, and even within the minds of individuals.

Rather than seek an agreed international definition of terrorism, it may be more profitable to do what the criminal codes of individual countries already do anyway: to define particular prohibited acts, ranging from acts threatening the public order all the way to murder. In fact it is through such national legislation in different states that all legal prosecutions for terrorist actions actually take place, though often thanks to the collaboration of police forces and other agencies from several states.

The foregoing discussion suggests that 'terrorism' can come in many forms: internal, international, governmental, non-governmental, crypto-governmental, and so on. It may be one component of a basically political struggle, it may be seen as no more than a response to an adversary's terrorism, or it may for that matter degenerate into criminality. There is not necessarily anything wrong with calling all of these things 'terrorism'. However, there should be no illusions that such nomenclature will be widely—let alone universally—accepted, or that it will aid our understanding of the causes of this disturbing phenomenon, or enable us to oppose it effectively.

(2) Has there been an increase in terrorism?

The sense that terrorism is on the increase, and that international action alone can stop it, was well conveyed even before the 1986 Tokyo summit in the following statement:

> The past year has been remarkable for the number and grave character of the outrages which have been accomplished or attempted abroad, in furtherance of political, social, industrial, or personal objects. At no former period of our experience have there been so many desperate attempts—some of them only too fatally successful—to destroy life and property by means of dynamite and similar explosives. There is only one gratifying consideration in connection with the long and dreary list of these outrages, and that is, that the frequency and cosmopolitan charac-ter of crimes of this sort probably bring us so much nearer to the time when an international agreement will be arrived at whereby criminals of this class will, like pirates, be treated as enemies of the human race, and pursued with relentless vigour from country to country, and debarred from shelter or sympathy in any part of the civilized world, and this without reference to whether the actuating motive was political, industrial or other. Indeed, it is difficult to understand how any motive can be deemed to sanctify or palliate so horrible and dastardly a form of offence, one of the most deplorable features of which, as we have before remarked, is the callous indifference to whether the consequences fall on persons wholly innocent of any participation in, and unconnected with, the particular matter or cause against which the crime is directed.[8]

That was written in 1892. It is indeed the case that upsurges in terrorist activity worldwide have occurred at various times before now, and most notably in the period 1969–71. The fact that such upsurges occur may confirm the view that there is an imitative element in terrorist activity; and it may help justify the belief that terrorism should be tackled as a global phenomenon, rather than treated as the outgrowth of individual societies or the consequence of particular injustices.

It is not so clear that there has been a general increase in terrorist activity in 1985–6, as the Tokyo declaration on terrorism claimed. What there may have been is an increase in terrorist attacks directed at particular targets—including India on account of Sikh troubles; and the USA with the involvement of its citizens in the *Achille Lauro* affair in October 1985, in the attacks on Rome and Vienna airports on 27 December 1985, and in the Berlin discotheque attack.

As far as these attacks on US targets are concerned, they were in fact much less costly in American lives than some incidents in preceding years—such as the lorry bomb in Beirut in October 1983 which killed 260 US servicemen. One can speculate that the terrorist attacks of 1985–6 attracted the attention they did (a) because they were directed against some totally defenceless targets, most clearly symbolized by Mr Leon Klinghoffer in his wheelchair on the *Achille Lauro*; (b) because of the substantial evidence of involvement of a small state, Libya, which the USA has in any case ample reason to dislike; and (c) because President Reagan has persistently proclaimed as an aim of his administration the defeat of international terrorism. A further consideration in the minds of US policy-makers may have been evidence that other terrorist attacks were planned, and foiled, in early 1986.

(3) Attempts at justifying terrorism

The Tokyo declaration says clearly that terrorism has no justification. Plainly this does not mean that justifications of terrorism have not been put forward—only that they are viewed as inadequate. The way the statement is formulated, however, gives no clue that the various attempted justifications of terrorism have been taken at all seriously.

The long history of terrorism is littered with elaborate attempts at justification.[9] Many, but by no means all, hinge on the idea of terrorism as justified counterviolence. Terrorism is seen as a necessary response to the use of terror or violence in some form by an adversary; and is allegedly the best way to bring about a more just order. In other words, what we call terrorism is seen as counterterrorism—and vice versa.

Such attempts at justifying terrorism are often plainly inadequate. For example, it is notorious that theories of 'structural violence' imply in a suspiciously facile way that because a given governmental system is by nature violent and oppressive, counterviolence against it is necessarily justified. In fact it is all too likely that the counterviolence will merely mean that a society is burdened with two terrorisms instead of one—with each living off the other in a symbiotic relationship.

Overall, the record of terrorism in the past two centuries is not one to inspire confidence in it as a method. It has often failed completely to achieve anything like the intended results; led to massive public revulsion against the methods employed; degenerated, like the Mafia, into little more than criminality; or, as in Cyprus, Lebanon and elsewhere, led to intercommunal violence and paved the way for foreign intervention.

However, there are instances in which it is plainly not enough for governments to condemn terrorism or deny that it has any justification. Such an approach can appear to treat a deep historical tragedy as if it were a mere behavioural problem. In October 1985 and early 1986 the British government sought to discuss Middle Eastern problems with various PLO representatives on condition that they renounced violence. Similar conditions appear to have been made with the African National Congress (ANC) in respect of South African problems, and then dropped. Even if such attempts were to succeed, as the PLO ones almost did, in the sense that the condition was met and the discussions went ahead, it is doubtful whether an extracted promise to pursue a peaceful resolution would do very much more than isolate those who made it. There may be more merit in some cases in accepting that some justifications for some kinds of guerrilla violence, however one may view them oneself, are serious and run deep.

(4) The 'terrorist state'

The Tokyo declaration put notable emphasis on the idea that terrorist states exist and ought to be isolated. In the declaration, a series of measures was proposed 'in respect of any state which is clearly involved in sponsoring or supporting international terrorism, and in particular of Libya, until such time as the state concerned abandons its complicity in, or support for, such terrorism.'

Because of the notorious difficulties of defining terrorism, which is almost as difficult as defining aggression, statements such as this only have any substantial meaning to the extent that individual countries can be named—as in this case Libya was. In this sense, the British and American delight that Libya was named in the declaration was understandable, especially since there is a great deal of evidence of various kinds of Libya's involvement in many kinds of terrorist acts far from its own territory.

There are, however, dangers in the contemporary preoccupation with the 'terrorist state'. (a) The evidence of state involvement in terrorist acts is usually by nature ambiguous. (b) A very large number of states have been accused in recent years of sponsoring and supporting international terrorism, including the Soviet Union, Syria, Nicaragua and the USA. In many cases it simply is not practical to respond to such accusations (assuming them to be well founded) by implementing mechanically a predetermined list of measures, and the effectiveness of such measures if implemented may be doubted. Still less would it be appropriate in all cases to respond by punitive measures, such as bombing. (c) The state which engages in support for one terrorist cause may itself be a valued partner in some other activities—not just in trade, but also in matters relating to international security, even in the control of some forms of terrorism.

Above all, preoccupation with the idea of the 'terrorist state' as the *fons et origo* of terrorism may serve to obscure the other causes of this phenomenon, and may also lead to a search for the easy target. Libya is a much easier state to punish than is Syria or the Soviet Union. Unless great care is exercised in addressing the question of terrorist states, there is a risk that democratic governments may be at least partially vulnerable to the same accusation as terrorists themselves: of going for the easy targets.

Despite these dangers, any state which does engage in extensive support of terrorist activities abroad cannot expect necessarily to be able to take advantage of all the normal privileges and immunities of states. There is likely to come a point at which other states feel the need to take action against it—though exactly what kind of action is appropriate in the circumstances is bound to be a matter requiring very careful judgment.

(5) The struggle against terrorism

Views about the means by which the struggle against terrorism should be conducted generally polarize around two approaches. They can be roughly categorized as (a) the police plus non-violent sanctions approach, and (b) the military approach.

The first approach stresses that what defeats terrorism in the end is slow, patient police work: foiling plots, defusing bombs, arresting and trying culprits, diplomatic expulsions and the like: supplemented, perhaps, by economic or other boycotts of an offending state.

The second approach stresses that terrorism deserves in addition a more violent response—though one which is more carefully targeted and discriminate than the terrorist acts complained of. The bombing of targets in Tripoli and Benghazi on the night of 14–15 April 1986 was justified by the American and British governments in these terms.

These are not the only possible or actual approaches to terrorism. There remains a need, for example, for more use of political persuasion to point out to potential terrorists (some of whom have motives more respectable than their methods) the strength of the arguments against the use of terrorism: its tendency to backfire, to spread, to lead both to a strong reaction and to the destruction of society through the increase of unauthorized violence. There is a need, too, to remind potential terrorists and their sympathizers that there are other means of pursuing their objects—means which vary from case to case, and may include constitutional action, non-violent struggle, or even possibly in some cases disciplined military struggle against legitimate targets.

It is noteworthy that in the current international climate, in which both superpowers subscribe to anti-colonial ideologies, no one proposes that there should be an overt military takeover of a state which is perceived as delinquent. Thus the options open to the international community to influence events in Libya are distinctly limited. All involve some element of remote control.

The first approach outlined above—the police plus non-violent sanctions one—is widely supported, though with different degrees of conviction as to its adequacy. Even many who incline very strongly to this view do not by any means reject all military action: they may well favour, for example, commando raids to release hostages, or to seize hijackers.

The second approach—the military one—is obviously more controversial, and for very good reasons. The record of what might be termed cross-border, military-punitive responses to terrorist actions is not a particularly encouraging one. Taken at its most extreme, there is a risk that such actions will themselves be misinterpreted by the intended victims or by third parties as aggressive threats, and that they will make violence worse, not better. The classic example of this is the Austrian determination in July 1914 to destroy the Serbian 'hornets' nest' following the assassination of Archduke Ferdinand at Sarajevo, the capital of Bosnia, on 28 June 1914. This led directly to the outbreak of World War I. In our own time, the dismal consequences of the June 1982 Israeli invasion of Lebanon, which Israel justified as 'an exercise of its legitimate right of self-defence' in response to terrorist attacks, serves as a reminder of the potentially destructive consequences of the military-punitive approach.[10]

A particular difficulty with the military-punitive approach is that both its motives and its consequences are so easily misinterpreted. An action by one great power may be intended as totally defensive in character, but it can only too easily happen that a rival great power interprets the same action as an extension of power, a threat to itself, or a challenge to its credibility as an ally. Fortunately there was little likelihood that the Soviet Union would act on the basis of such an interpretation of the US attacks on Libya: although the Soviet Union has supplied Libya extensively with arms, it has long been nervous about many aspects of Colonel Gaddafi's policies; so its support contains an element of limited liability over and above that element of caution which often characterizes Soviet involvements overseas. However, the risk that the Soviet Union might feel humiliated by attacks on friendly states, and hence seek to assert its authority in some sphere or another, probably remains.

There is another problem with the military-punitive approach: that it may lead to a general decline in international standards. Thus it is not surprising that just five weeks after the US raid on Libya of 14–15 April 1986, South African forces attacked a series of targets in Zambia, Zimbabwe and Botswana, claiming that they were 'terrorist centres'. In such circumstances the South African authorities could presumably be confident that the USA would not be in a strong position to take them to task for their action.

A final problem of the military-punitive approach has to do with the choice of targets. It is not at all easy to select suitable targets for military raids, since relatively few targets are clearly and indisputably associated with terrorism. There is bound to be a tendency to aim for the responsible head of government—and it is obvious that this may have been one aim of the US raid of 14–15 April 1986. Yet any assumption that if only the head of government can be killed, things will improve, is precisely the assumption made by many nineteenth- and twentieth-century terrorists themselves. It proved spectacularly wrong in Tsarist Russia, and indeed elsewhere. It would be deeply ironic if it were to be reincarnated in the name of counterterrorism. Yet there are signs of this: after the Israeli bombing of the PLO headquarters near Tunis on 1 October 1985, the Israeli Chief of Staff confirmed that Mr Arafat had been a target of the raid.[11]

Because of considerations such as these, there has been a long tradition of scepticism about punitive raids as a reprisal for terrorism. The United States government was often in the past sceptical, or even openly critical, of such raids, and made its views on this point known to France during the Algerian war, for example in 1958, the time of various incidents involving Algeria and Tunisia. Then, at the time of European involvement against anti-colonial rebels, it was the European powers who favoured punitive raids and the Americans who counselled patience and caution. Now the boot is on the other foot. However, the very threat of international disorder implicit in the April 1986 US raid on Libya may, paradoxically, have spurred other states to take the matter of non-violent sanctions more seriously—which they did, for example, at the Tokyo summit.

The legal justifications which were produced for the US raid of 14–15 April 1986 call for comment. Clearly an air raid in what is more than just notionally peacetime, on targets in cities in a sovereign state, is something which takes a great deal of justifying. The normal presumption is bound to be that such acts are a departure from established international practice and from basic rules of international law. An attempt could have been made to justify the action in the rather debatable terms of the body of international law governing reprisals—that is, otherwise illegal acts of retaliation carried out in response to illegal acts of warfare and intended to cause the enemy to comply with the law. Whether this approach was considered or not is not known. Factors militating against this approach may have included the unsatisfactory and contested state of the law governing reprisals;[12] the poor record of reprisals by Israel against terrorist acts; and the fact that the United States and Libya, despite the occasional hostilities between them, are not in a state of war.

In the event the legal justification advanced by the USA was 'the inherent right of individual or collective self-defence if an armed attack occurs against a member of the United Nations', as spelt out in Article 51 of the United Nations Charter. This was similar to the legal case made by Israel in respect of its 1982 invasion of Lebanon. There was a great deal of questioning by international lawyers and others as to whether the meaning of Article 51 could really be stretched to include a situation where the armed attack was not against the territory of the USA, but only against some of its citizens abroad; where the delay between the offending attack and the US response was not used to present all the evidence to international bodies (including the Security Council) in order to try to get them to act; and where the raid itself resulted in a greater loss of life than the acts complained of. Such worries would no doubt be viewed by the US government as legalistic quibbles, of a kind which will be quickly forgotten. But they reflect a real and widespread concern to maintain the existing, albeit fragile, barriers against the endless extension of the use of force.

The judgment of the International Court of Justice on the merits of *Nicaragua v. USA*, announced on 27 June 1986, confirms the importance of exercising care in all aspects of a decision about use of force against what is perceived as a delinquent state. Although the facts of the case are different from those involved in the US-Libya conflict, the Court's carefully reasoned judgment in the Nicaragua case does point to the importance of certain general factors relating to the use of force, including:

(1) While the general rule prohibiting the use of force does allow for exceptions in the case of self-defence, whether the response to the attack is lawful depends on observance of the criteria of the necessity and the proportionality of the measures taken in self-defence (paragraph 194).

(2) If self-defence is advanced as a justification for measures which would otherwise be in breach both of the principle of customary international law and of that contained in the UN Charter, it is to be expected that the conditions of the Charter, that measures should be 'immediately reported' to the Security Council, should be respected (paragraphs 200 and 235).

(3) If a plea of collective self-defence is made, it is important that the alleged victims of aggression actually request military help (paragraphs 232–4, 238 and 246).

(4) The provisions of the laws of war (i.e. international humanitarian law governing the conduct of armed conflicts) need to be observed strictly (paragraphs 215–20 and 254–6).[13]

The fact that in its struggle against what it perceives as a delinquent state the USA has had to be reminded of these rather basic considerations is alarming—as, too, was the US withdrawal from the case. If the struggle against terrorism is to be effectively conducted, it can only be on the basis of a serious attempt at broadly-based multilateral cooperation. That in turn necessitates acting in such a way as to command a reasonable measure of international support.

Notes

1. Menachem Begin, *The Revolt*, rev. edn (W.H. Allen, London 1979), p. 59.
2. See, for example, the discussion of these issues in Nathan Leites, *The Vietcong Style of Politics*, Rand Memorandum RM-5487-1-ISA/ARPA (Rand Corporation, Santa Monica, CA, 1969). He suggests that terror was not on its own an adequate basis of control; a sense of the moral justice of the cause was also present. The two factors were mutually reinforcing.
3. See Robert Conquest, *The Great Terror: Stalin's Purge of the Thirties* (Macmillan, London, 1968).
4. See, for example, Eugene V. Walter, *Terror and Resistance: A Study of Political Violence with Case Studies of Some Primitive African Communities* (Oxford University Press, New York, 1969).
5. Milovan Djilas, *The New Class: An Analysis of the Communist System*, Unwin Book No. 68 (Allen & Unwin, London, 1966), pp. 145–6.
6. Of course some parts of the 1974 UN Definition of Aggression, Article 3, might be quoted to greater or lesser effect against states taking counterterrorist action. Acts qualifying as aggression include 'Bombardment by the armed forces of a State against the territory of another State' (paragraph b); and 'the action of a State in allowing its territory, which it has placed at the disposal of another State, to be used by that other State for perpetrating an act of aggression against a third State' (paragraph f).
7. Hijacking of aircraft is addressed in the Tokyo (1963), Hague (1970) and Montreal (1971) conventions on civil aviation. These require states either to extradite or to prosecute hijackers. Not all states have become parties to, or are willing to observe the terms of, these agreements.
8. Col. V.D. Majendie, CB, HM Chief Inspector of Explosives, in the Report of the HMCIE, in 1892.

9. On the tangled history of thought about the subject, see especially Walter Laqueur, *Terrorism* (Weidenfeld & Nicolson, London, 1977).
10. The quotation is from a statement issued by the Embassy of Israel, London, 18 June 1982.
11. One way in which counterterrorist action may itself degenerate into terrorism is described in George Jonas, *Vengeance: The True Story of an Israeli Counter-terrorist Mission* (Collins, London, 1984). This book claims to give the inside story of an Israeli hit squad which was active in Europe and in Lebanon between 1972 and 1974, following the massacre of Israeli athletes at the 1972 Munich Olympics. My view is that the book is consonant with known facts and probably genuine.
12. On which, see especially Frits Kalshoven, *Belligerent Reprisals* (Sijthoff, Leyden, 1971).
13. International Court of Justice, *Military and Paramilitary Activities In and Against Nicaragua (Nicaragua v. United States of America): Merits* (The Hague, 27 June 1986). This volume contains the full text of the Court's judgment and the various separate and dissenting opinions of individual judges.

3

The Middle East and terrorism

PHILIP WINDSOR

Why the Middle East?

A British Staff College recently held an international exercise in what it is now fashionable to call low-intensity operations. The scenario involved an attack by Arab terrorists; and one Arab participant was moved to protest. Why, he asked, could it not involve ETA or the IRA, if only for a change? He had a point, of course. Terrorism is now so widespread as a method of political action, or as reaction to political failure, that a very large proportion of the countries in the world have to confront it in one form or another. It extends from Canada to Sri Lanka, from Japan to the leading countries of Western Europe, and one might well argue that there is nothing special about its manifestations in the Middle East. But there are in fact considerations which make the Middle East a particular case.

These considerations are of two kinds. The first relates to the question of whether terrorism is endemic in the politics of the Middle East. This clearly is not the place to go back to the Hashashin, the historical and etymological ancestors of today's assassins, or to their remote and semi-mythological overlord, the Old Man of the Mountains, who evoked such dread among the Crusaders. But their Shi'ite descendants have certainly been active in the few years that have elapsed since the Israeli invasion of the

Lebanon, and have moreover inspired awe, respect or fear in different Arab circles—not only by their readiness to commit martyrdom, but also by their ability to achieve what the Palestine Liberation Organization has promised ever since 1967 but has never carried out: namely, to drive the Israelis out of territories they had occupied by force. There is, in other words, a terrorist tradition in the politics of the Middle East. It is far from being the only tradition in the political culture of the Arab world (and in any case all political cultures contain conflicting and frequently contradictory tendencies), but it has a long ancestry. When Arab political leaders invoke the example, as they so frequently do, of the Crusader state as a precedent for the future fate of Israel, they are in part referring to that tradition. Such organizations as the Hezbollah do so out loud.

In most other parts of the world, by contrast, terrorism is an explicitly modern phenomenon. It, too, has a certain ancestry—one has only to read Dostoevsky or Conrad—but the point at issue here is twofold. First, terrorist actions have generally been, until recently, relatively discriminating. The famous case of the Russian terrorist who, out to get the Grand Duke Nicholas, instead allowed himself to be arrested bomb in hand because the Duchess unexpectedly formed part of the company, would not have been recognizable to any terrorist of today. Second, even limited terrorism had almost died out in the Western world, and in many other areas of the globe which had been under its control, until comparatively recently. The IRA has existed since the civil conflicts which surrounded the birth of the Irish Republic, but it was not until 1969 that the Provisionals began their campaign; and such attacks as the IRA had carried out itself in the intervening years were largely symbolic. In this sense, and in most contemporary societies, terrorism has emerged as a new and specific phenomenon, particularly in its indiscriminate form. In the Middle East, by contrast, there is continuity as well as tradition. The hapless British soldiery in Mandate Palestine were subject to attacks, both during and after World War II, from Jewish terrorist organizations like Irgun Zvai Leumi and the Stern Gang, as well as from less organized Arab extremists. Indeed, one might argue that the whole melancholy history of Palestine did much to legitimize the modern phenomenon of terrorism in the Middle East, and that in that sense the more activist elements of the PLO are merely following in the footsteps of the man who later became the Prime

Minister of Israel and denounced the PLO in its entirety as a bunch of thugs and murderers.

The name of Palestine raises the second kind of consideration. Obviously, not all terrorism is domestically based. Canadians have to watch out for Sikhs. But, for the most part, the proliferation of terrorism in the contemporary world is related to domestic conflicts. It is indeed the Sikh-Hindu relationship in India which has spilled over into Canadian politics, and the Singhalese-Tamil relationship in Sri Lanka which affects the governability of India. The effects of terrorism are by no means domestically confined; but, generally speaking, its causes are domestic—even if the *domus* in question happens to be the arbitrary and ethnically mixed remnant of a colonial past.

In the case of the Middle East, however, terrorism acquired an international dimension, was indeed based in international politics, from the beginning. The history of Mandate Palestine is the history of a struggle for the international definition of a future entity, very different from that, say, of ethnic divisions in the island of Ceylon. The history of relations between the state of Israel and its Arab neighbours is, obviously, an international history—and one which progressed through acts of terrorism. The *fedayeen* raids on Israel in the early years of the state's existence were sponsored neither by Egypt nor by Jordan—indeed, both went to considerable lengths to try to prevent them—but in the end they led to the Israeli assault on Gaza in 1955. In response to that, Egypt did lend active encouragement to the *fedayeen*, so indicating that in the international politics of the Middle East it was now possible for some states to conduct their relations through terrorist acts. In turn, such activities helped to produce the Suez war of 1956.

It is in the politics of the Middle East that terrorism first became an international concern, and an activity with completely disproportionate and unpredictable consequences. It is equally the case that more than one party to the Arab-Israeli dispute is capable of sponsoring terrorism. Syria has certainly done so on occasion; but some of the activities of the Israeli retaliatory force, the notorious Unit 101, could also be regarded as state-sponsored terrorism. It is finally in the politics of the Middle East today that carefully assembled acts of diplomacy and intricate calculations as to how the process of peacemaking might be advanced can be totally jeopardized by a wanton act of terrorism, as in the hijacking of the cruise liner *Achille Lauro* in autumn 1985. This is a point which deserves further consideration, but in the meantime one might remark that just as it was the Middle East which made terrorism an international concern, so it is also the Middle East which is uniquely vulnerable to the international effects of a single terrorist exploit.

The contemporary sources

It is obvious that the major source of Middle Eastern terrorism today lies in the unresolved Palestinian problem. The dispersal of the Palestinians, coupled with the failure of one peace process after another, has meant a proliferation of groups and organizations dedicated to terrorist action against Israel and by extension the United States. But this is not to say that such bodies, normally but not universally affiliated to the PLO, represent the only forms of Middle Eastern terrorism. There are two other major kinds of terrorist activity.

The first lies in attempts made by the PLO, not to strike at Israel, but to gain some degree of independent political power at the expense of a host country. Efforts of this kind were reflected in the spate of international hijackings and murders-on-the-spot which preceded King Hussein's decision to crack down on the PLO in September 1970. A similar power struggle was going on in the Lebanon before the Israeli invasion of June 1982. And the name of Lebanon also points to the other form of terrorism.

No doubt the PLO provided an inspiration and example for a manifold set of groupings—whether sectarian or simple ethnic minorities. But such groupings already existed and had in the past resorted to terrorism at least on occasion, just as they would do again. Many were concentrated in the Lebanon, but others had roots in several countries. The Muslim Brotherhood is one such. And the Lebanon itself offers an extraordinarily ambiguous case.

As the workings of the Constitution came under increasing pressure, both from the Palestinian presence and from the growth of sectarian and minority discontent, so the old *Zaim* system (that is, the traditional system of feudatory families on which the Lebanese polity has long been based) became increasingly prominent in the management of Lebanese affairs. A number of the various families concerned also became increasingly antagonistic to each other—in terms which offered a field-day to their respective militias. In itself, this does not imply terrorism. Street-fighting, and Lilliputian campaigns in the mountains, might cost a lot of lives, but these are lost in open battle. Moreover, such fighting is discriminatory in the sense that the militias' targets are each other, not bystanders, peasants and families. But the ambiguity arises when such feudatory rivalries adopt the measures of kidnapping and murder. In that manner, ancient but relatively contained animosities can rapidly turn into contemporary forms of terrorism which, as they spiral in intensity, can lead to massacres on a large scale. This happened in the Lebanon. It also encouraged the spread of terrorist activity to other groups which had in the past seldom aspired to take part in traditional power struggles. Among these were elements of the Shi'ite population.

In general, it might be said that the Palestinian problem and the activities of some terrorist organizations within the PLO have interacted with more traditional forms of enmity, especially in the Lebanon, to produce a new and lethal mixture. To this one must add the spread of militant Shi'ism, not only in the Lebanon, but also in other parts of the Middle East: Bahrein, Kuwait, and who knows where next?

While, therefore, the Palestinian problem is undoubtedly the source of the recrudescence of terrorism in Middle Eastern politics, there is nonetheless more than one brand of terrorism, just as there are several different kinds of international conflict which terrorism can engender. Iranian attempts to export God all over the Gulf and beyond, the international ramifications of the activities of the Muslim Brotherhood, the relations between warring Christians, Palestinians and Syrians—all these form as much a part of the ghastly international tapestry as do the activities of certain PLO groupings. Meanwhile, PLO exploits at sea, in Cyprus and Malta, or in the air, attract Israeli reprisals, even as far afield as Tunis. But the Greeks had a word for it. The pattern of outrage and reprisal ensures that terrorism is hydra-headed; and that every act of massive retaliation or every demonstration of American determination to stamp out terrorism will only produce more terrorists. Their group-ings are increasingly likely to be small, obscure, virtually untrace-able, with no particular political programme or state sponsor, and inspired only by a desire for revenge or even a straightforwardly psychotic determination to make a mark in the world.

Terrorism threatens to become an autonomous activity, not linked to its sources in the Palestinian problem or in any other religious or ideological competition. The real danger that states must confront when dealing with the question of terrorism is not so much whether other states encourage it in the hope of achieving some objective, but whether it can turn into terrorism for terrorism's sake. To some extent, this has already happened.

Some principal organizations

The PLO has never been a coherent organization: it is a congeries of different and frequently antagonistic groups, all using the same flag for an umbrella. But it was also the case that a leadership structure had been established in the largest and most important group, el-Fatah, and that many of its leaders were willing to accept at least a regime of peaceful coexistence with Israel, based on Israeli withdrawal from Gaza and the West Bank. That was the case before the invasion of the Lebanon in June 1982. But the Israeli achievement in driving the PLO out of Beirut, like the subsequent Syrian achievement in driving it out of Tripoli, has merely ensured that the PLO leadership is now so scattered and so insecure that it cannot control the activities of those who desire to indulge in terrorism—if only as a challenge to the leadership itself.

The defeat of the PLO in the Lebanon, and its subsequent dispersal among eight Arab countries, have resulted in what one might politely call a structural reorganization of the PLO or, more realistically, its disintegration. The rebellion of May 1983 in Fatah's own ranks against Yassir Arafat's leadership, which was led by 'Abu Moussa' with Syrian backing, has meant a continuing power struggle in the Lebanon, in which not only Palestinian and Syrian forces have been involved, but also, at different times, those of the Druse and the Amal militia. The real point underlying this struggle is that the Palestinians in the major camps remain on the whole loyal to Arafat, whatever the intermittent carnage, and will therefore continue to provide a focus for terrorism.

In the wider Lebanese arena, the struggle is also influenced by the growing activities of the Hezbollah in the Beka'a Valley and in the southwest. During 1986 Syria in fact withdrew nearly three-quarters of its troops from the Beka'a, and it became clear that its role in the

Lebanon was radically diminished. The irony here is that Syria, which has certainly sponsored terrorism in the past, and particularly during the period of the Israeli withdrawal from Lebanese territory, now finds it difficult to master the forces it helped unleash. It is no more the hegemon in the Lebanon than Israel could be—and in both cases the failure is in good part due to terrorists. (For this purpose one might lump in the Iranian Revolutionary Guards, who are also active in the Beka'a, along with the Hezbollah.) In an interview with the *Washington Post* shortly after the American raids on Libya, President Assad declared that he was no longer capable of controlling terrorism in the Lebanon. Considering that very shortly before this President Reagan had declared that if there were evidence of Syrian involvement in terrorism the United States would take retaliatory action, Assad's statement was well-timed. But that does not make it untrue; and, internationally, he certainly made some efforts in the same period to distance himself from Iran.

The result of the split within Fatah was that on the one hand Yassir Arafat was driven to intensify his efforts to join the peace process alongside King Hussein (until it broke down in February 1986) and that, on the other, a number of attacks on Israeli citizens and targets were carried out, apparently by members of the Arafat faction. What is quite unclear is whether this was done on the orders of the leadership, whether a blind eye was as good as a nod, or whether the attacks represented a limited attempt to sabotage any incipient peace process. What seems certain is that a power struggle was involved between 'Force 17', from which Arafat's personal bodyguard is drawn, and the 'Western Sector' under the command of the old PLO war-pony 'Abu Jihad'.

Officially, Israelis tend to argue that such actions demonstrate that any PLO commitment to a peace process is inherently untrustworthy and that the mask of public diplomacy still hides the faces of those bent on murder. On the public evidence, such a possibility cannot be ruled out—but it does presuppose an organizational cohesion and a political coherence which seem to be notably lacking in the counsels of the PLO. Before the Israeli invasion of the Lebanon, a truce negotiated the previous year by Mr Philip Habib, the special American envoy, had held good for nearly a twelvemonth. (Indeed, it was broken, not by any grouping affiliated to the PLO, but by one of the most shadowy and sinister of the autonomous organizations mentioned above, the 'Abu Nidal' group. And it was broken, not from Lebanese territory, but in London.) It would be impossible to imagine such a degree of control in the circumstances which have prevailed since the invasion.

In this context, it is worth considering again the case of the *Achille Lauro* already mentioned. It was an earthquake in the politics of the Middle Eastern peace process, first because it seemed to demonstrate either that Arafat could not control his followers or else that he was engaged in a game of bloody duplicity; and, second, because the reactions to the event strained relations between the United States and Egypt almost to a critical point of tension, and left those between the United States and Italy exceedingly sour. More than any other single event, it cast doubt on the credibility of the peace process at a crucial moment.

It appears to have been carried out by certain members of the 'Abul Abbas' faction, which is normally loyal to Arafat; but whether his complicity, or those of his immediate aides, is thereby implied is an entirely open question. In this sense, the *Achille Lauro* incident exemplifies to a high degree the sheer uncertainty which surrounds, not only the motives and nature of terrorism in Middle Eastern politics, but also the relationship between terrorism and negotiations.

Meanwhile, the traditionally 'radical' elements of the PLO—the PDFLP under Naif Hawatmeh, the PFLP under Georges Habash, and the PFLP General Command under Ahmad Jibril—continue to find bases of support in either Syria (PDFLP), or Libya (PFLP and PFLP-GC), or in some other cases both. Libya also gives succour to the 'Abu Nidal' movement, otherwise known as Black June, which is effectively an anti-PLO organization as much as it is officially an anti-Israeli one; and which, according to recent Israeli reports, has now joined forces with the Arab Liberation Front which operates in Jordan—and is in itself even more anti-Jordanian than it is anti-Israeli.

This is only a very sketchy indication of some of the forces at work and of the marked fluidity of the situation which has developed from the disintegration of the PLO structure. But two considerations arise.

The first is that certain states which have in the past sponsored a fair amount of terrorism, such as Syria in particular, might now find that they have to draw in their horns. Terrorist activities are no longer necessarily conducive to even the more ruthless calculations of what constitutes *raison d'état*. It falls to Libya to shelter most forms of Palestinian-based terrorism, just as it does to Iran to foster most forms of extreme Shi'ite terror. These two are in fact the only true examples of the phenomenon frequently referred to as the 'maverick state'. That is a point to return to.

The second consideration involved here is that much Middle Eastern terrorism is not directed at Israelis or Americans *per se*, or even at people checking in their luggage at European airports. Such bystanders might provide convenient targets, while Israeli or American deaths might, in the eyes of some at least, serve to legitimize an outrage. But the real *objectives*, as opposed to the actual *targets*, of terrorist activities frequently relate to internal power struggles, to factional disputes and ideological disagreements rather than to any sense of how to achieve political aims or carry on a perverted crusade. In this context, the point is worth making again that punishing host states does very little to curb the growth of terrorism.

Will it spread?

Terrorism has in the recent past frequently been associated with the idea of the maverick state as sponsor. But what is a maverick state? Presumably, it is one which has no interest in an existing international order and which sees no future in such a framework. As a fideistic entity, Iran might be held to be one of those; and, as a country thoroughly disappointed by the politics of Arab nationalism as well as one which carries a deep sense of humiliation into the wider international sphere, Libya is another.

Libya under Muammar Gaddafi is the embodiment of the maverick state. Gaddafi himself is fairly representative of a certain kind of Arab male: one whose enthusiasm for what he accepts as traditional values is matched by an obscure understanding of the need to embrace modernity if he or his country is to cut a figure in the world. At the same time, such a combination leads to intellectual perplexity and psychological insecurity—whether about the relations between men and women, or about those between Islam and socialism. The Green Book attests to all that. But his attempts to formulate a synthesis within the framework of the Arab nation—and more widely within that of the Islamic *ummah* (the community of Islam)—have met with little but rebuff, except from those who

34

were willing to accept his oil money. Humiliated by the history of Libya's relations with the West, conscious of the past glories and more recent ineffectiveness of Arab civilization, he is equally disappointed by the failure of the contemporary Arab state system to respond to his visions. This helps to make of him not only a natural sponsor of radical Palestinian groupings, which do not represent a state so much as an aspiration, but also a natural enemy of the wider international order.

Syria, on the other hand, is very much a state which has been trying to advance its influence and interests within the existing framework. President Assad has certainly sponsored terrorism, but he has done so in a controlled and calculating manner. (He has on occasion also helped keep it within bounds: it is perhaps worth recalling that his intervention was decisive in saving those aboard the TWA airliner hijacked to Beirut in the summer of 1985.) He knows very well where Syria's interests lie, and he can be utterly ruthless in pursuing them; but he is no more the leader of a maverick state than was any Borgia or heartless Florentine.

In other words, there is no necessary correspondence between a support for terrorism and the question of whether a state is 'maverick' or not. But what is clear is that unless the international framework itself can provide some way of addressing grievances, resolving disputes, and providing for the legitimate security concerns of antagonistic entities, the role of the maverick state and the incidence of terrorism are both likely to grow. When the peace process between Israel and its neighbours, which King Hussein had been painfully trying to pursue for nearly three and a half years, collapsed in February 1986, it became clear that the international framework was unlikely to fulfil any of these functions. The king himself has certainly voiced the fear that, however tenuous the process might have been, its collapse would lead to a radicalization of Arab youth, an exponential growth in terrorism, and new and dangerous forms of interaction between Palestinian and Shi'ite extremism.

Whether his more despairing anticipations are confirmed or not, they do suggest that terrorism is not a phenomenon which can simply be isolated and dealt with accordingly—particularly not in the Middle East. Experiences have already shown how Middle Eastern terrorism can affect East-West and West-West relations. It can also destabilize the region, with far graver consequences than anything encountered hitherto. That might especially be the case if, as now seems possible, it acquires or becomes an ethos of its own.

In the end, there are two ways of dealing with terrorism. One is to attempt to deal with the phenomenon itself—to adopt a policy of punishment or hitting back. Israel has done this for many years, even though not always consistently; and the United States was proclaiming a similar resolve when it bombed Benghazi and Tripoli. The historical evidence does not suggest that this is a very effective mode of procedure; indeed, if anything is to be learnt, it is that such methods are merely likely to produce more terrorists. The other way is to try to tackle the root cause of the phenomenon, and of the problems it creates in relations between states and peoples. In the case of the Middle East, that means a serious and sustained attempt to find an answer to the Palestinian question—overladen with complexities and ambiguities as that admittedly is. Even if an answer were to be found, it is possible that certain forms of terrorism could survive, as they also have elsewhere, but at least they would be cut off from that basis of popular support which makes the politics of the Middle East so problematic and frequently so bloody today. And, in such a context, to cut terrorism off from popular support is probably the best that can be hoped for. Diplomacy might be able to accomplish that. Air raids cannot.

4

Trends in international terrorism and the American response

PAUL WILKINSON

Problems of definition

The problem of definition has bedevilled public debate and informed analysis concerning terrorism. This is evident from the confused commentary in the more sensational literature on the subject.[1] In recent years, however, a surprisingly broad consensus has emerged in the academic usage of the term.[2] This recognizes that terrorism is a specific method of struggle rather than a synonym for political violence or insurgency. Brian Jenkins, in a television interview, aptly described it as a kind of weapons-system. It can be employed by an infinite variety of actors in the international system, including governments, political factions, criminal gangs, and even religious movements and cults. It is by no means the monopoly of any particular ideology, political philosophy or religion.

What distinguishes terrorism from other forms of violence is the deliberate and systematic use of coercive intimidation. For the politically motivated terrorist the object is generally to create a climate of fear among a wider target group than the immediate victims of the violence. Campaigns of terrorist violence can be used to publicize the terrorists' cause, as well as to coerce the wider target group to accede to the terrorists' aims. Thus there are at least five major groups of participants in the process of terror: the *perpetrators of the violence*; the *immediate victims*; the *wider target group*, or society, which the terrorists seek to intimidate; the *'neutral' bystanders* within the society experiencing the terrorism; and *international opinion*.

One obvious complication in applying this broad definition is that the use of terrorist violence is often interwoven with a wider repertoire of unconventional warfare. In Central America, for example, terrorism typically accompanies rural guerrilla activities and other forms of economic and political warfare. But in Western Europe and North America indigenous terrorism is usually seen in its 'pure' form: that is, unaccompanied by any wider insurgency. Terrorism is most easily identifiable when it is used by a weak and desperate minority, surrounded by an otherwise 'peaceful' society. A common feature of terrorist campaigns is that innocent civilians, sometimes foreign citizens who know nothing of the terrorists' political quarrel, are harmed. The typical weapons of the modern terrorist are explosive and incendiary bombings, shooting attacks and assassinations, hostage-taking and kidnapping, and hijackings.

Terrorism is clearly a very broad concept. Taxonomies and typologies of terrorism provide some helpful categories.[3] One basic distinction is between *state* and *factional* terror. In view of the sheer scale of crimes and mass terror against humanity that have been and are being committed by modern tyrannies, there should be no doubt that state terror is a far more severe and intractable problem for humanity than the containment and reduction of factional terror. This volume does not deal with the problems of internal terror by states. But we should recall that, historically, state terror has often been an antecedent to, and a contributory cause of, campaigns of factional terrorism. Once regimes assume that their ends justify any means, they tend to get locked into a spiral of terror and counterterror against their adversaries.

It is very important to distinguish between *international* and *internal* terrorism. Internal terrorism is systematic violence which is largely confined within a single state. International terrorism, in its most obvious manifestation, is a terrorist attack carried out across international frontiers or against a foreign target in the terrorist's state of origin. Yet in reality the international dimension often takes a more indirect form: a terrorist group may seek foreign cash, weapons, political support or other resources; its members and leaders may occasionally find safe havens abroad, or establish *ad hoc* cooperation with friendly foreign states and terrorist groups.

Historically, it is very hard to find a pure case of internal terrorism. After all, campaigns by the Provisional IRA in Northern Ireland and by ETA-militar in the Basque region of Spain constantly spill over their respective international frontiers and raise international problems of bilateral security cooperation and extradition. In this essay we will be considering only *international terrorism* and its implications, with references to internal terrorism when it clearly impinges upon the international system.

We can divide into at least five categories the perpetrators of international terrorism, by reference to their main declared aims and motives:

(1) *Nationalist terrorists.* These are groups seeking political self-determination. They may wage their struggle in the territory they seek to liberate and from bases abroad. Or, as in the cases of the Armenians and the Croatians, they may be forced by police action to campaign entirely in exile.

(2) *Ideological terrorists.* These groups profess to want to change the whole nature of the existing political, social and economic system. They have proved less durable than the well-established nationalist groups and are very prone to internal splits. Until comparatively recently they have been almost exclusively internal in character. However, since late 1984, a loose alliance of terrorist groups has emerged on the extreme left with the declared aim of striking at NATO and defence-related targets across Europe. Their activities are more coordinated than the occasional cooperation that existed between such groups in the 1970s.

(3) *Religious fanatics.* Certain religious groups employ international terrorism to undermine and ultimately overthrow a prevailing religious order which they regard as corrupt and evil. The best-known, and perhaps most feared, contemporary example is the Islamic Jihad group of fundamentalist Shi'ites, who have been inspired by the Iranian revolution and now challenge many of the moderate Arab regimes.

(4) *Single-issue fanatics.* These groups are obsessed with the desire to change a specific policy or practice within the target society. Examples are anti-nuclear, anti-abortion and 'animal rights'

extremists. There are some indications of international cooperation between the extreme anti-nuclear and 'ecological'
campaigners in Europe.

(5) *State-sponsored international terrorism.* This is used as a tool
both of domestic policy (e.g. Gaddafi's hit-squads sent abroad
to murder dissidents) and of foreign policy (e.g. Soviet
assistance to Palestinian extremists in the late 1970s and early
1980s designed to disrupt the Soviet Union's adversaries in the
Middle East). State sponsors may use their own directly
recruited and controlled terror squads, or may choose to work
through proxies and client movements. They almost invariably
work covertly in such support, in order plausibly to deny any
involvement.[4]

Before we leave the subject of definition and categories, it is
important to dispose of two surprisingly widespread misconceptions
about the term terrorism. First, it is sometimes objected that the
word terrorism should be abandoned because it is too value-laden. It
is a designation that most terrorists resist applying to themselves. Of
course it is true that anyone describing a particular campaign or act
of violence as terrorism is making a judgment, albeit about the
means used rather than the ends sought. But this does not mean that
we should jettison the term. Those who believe one can devise a
totally value-free language for the study of politics and society are
philosophically naive or disingenuous. Does any serious scholar
suggest we abandon terms such as 'dictatorship', 'imperialism' and
'democracy'?

A second widespread misunderstanding arises from the confusion
of means and ends. Whatever criteria we may choose for assessing
the legitimacy of a terrorist group to speak for a particular constituency, terrorists' claims to speak for even a bare majority of their
'own people' are largely unsustainable. Those few terrorist groups
that have, and take, the opportunity to form political parties and
fight elections often achieve derisory results. (The ideological and
religious fanatics do not even care about such tests of legitimacy
because they already believe that their belief-systems are superior to
all others and that these beliefs give them a transcendental justification for imposing their will by violence.) There may be a few clear
cases when we are persuaded that a terrorist group is motivated by a
legitimate grievance and can claim a degree of popular support

among its professed constituency. But does this mean we must refrain from designating any of their acts as terrorist? Surely not, because terrorism is not a philosophy or a movement: it is a method of struggle. There have been a number of historical cases where terrorism has been used on behalf of causes that most Western liberals would regard as just.

Any analysis of a specific terrorist campaign must, of course, take account of the specific political, historical and cultural context, and the ideology and aims of the groups involved. One needs to interpret the role and effectiveness of terrorism in the overall development of each conflict in which it appears. Is it being used as an auxiliary weapon in a wider strategy of revolutionary warfare? Or is it being used in isolation in a pre-insurgency mode? What degree of popular support, if any, do its perpetrators enjoy? How severe and prolonged is the violence? Is it merely spasmodic, and small in the scale and destruction caused? Or is it growing in intensity, frequency and lethality to the point at which it threatens to trigger a full-scale civil or international war?

The growth of modern international terrorism

There are certain conditions that explain the considerable growth in international terrorism indicated by the statistics in Table 4.1 (see statistical appendix at back of book). First, the general strategic situation favours unconventional war. The balance of terror, and the fact that all major states wish to avoid an escalation of violence that could lead to a possible nuclear conflict, are important factors. Most states today are afraid even of protracted and expensive conventional conflicts which might escalate. Unconventional war thus becomes relatively more attractive. In terms of cost-effectiveness, it may seem the best means of achieving political-diplomatic objectives by coercion.

The balance of terror is an important factor in the creation of a climate of thought about the use of violence as a mode of deterrence, as Lawrence Freedman argues in the next chapter. Some revolutionary movements see terror and the holding of hostages as the most appropriate weapons to use in microconflicts. Since the end of the struggles for colonial independence, national borders have become firmly established. It is now very difficult for any minority movement

41

to achieve a renegotiation of frontiers by diplomatic means. Hence the desperation, the argument from weakness mentioned earlier. Another factor is the psychology of relative deprivation—the feelings of political injustice felt by particular groups. Deep feelings of political injustice—deprivation of political rights or exclusion from power or influence within a community—can often lead to violent rebellion.

The weaknesses of both the international community and particular states in responding to terrorism also contributed to its increase. But since 1972 certain West European states have begun to take a firmer line; and there has been a widespread growth of elite units of special forces designed for hostage rescue, a development inspired by the success of the Entebbe (1976) and Mogadishu (1977) rescues. But since the TWA hijack to Beirut in 1985, and the disastrous loss of life in hijack to Malta in the same year, it has become clear that such rescue forces are not a panacea and do not necessarily restrain potential hijackers of the more fanatical type.

The shift of revolutionary theory in the Third World away from the rural guerrilla concept towards the idea of urban struggle is an important feature of contemporary terrorism. European revolutionaries in the nineteenth and early twentieth centuries had been through a similar process. The hunger for publicity—the propaganda of atrocity—tends to drive the modern revolutionary to the cities. As one of the leaders of the Algerian Front de Libération Nationale (FLN) put it, 'It was more effective propaganda to shoot a couple of French businessmen in the middle of Algiers than to shoot a hundred or so soldiers in a lonely gully.' Terrorism may even be contagious, in that communications can cause a bandwagon effect. Other factors precipitating the move to cities are technological opportunity and the vulnerability of industrial societies and cities to terrorist techniques. There is also the growth of ideologies and subcultures supportive of terrorism in some Western cities in the countries that had the highest numbers of terrorist attacks in the last decade. Finally, maverick states have been active in funding and giving sanctuary to terrorists.

These features characterize the international system of the late 1950s and 1960s. But from 1968 onwards there was an upsurge in modern international terrorism. It is generally agreed that two international developments had a key role in triggering this outbreak.

First was the overwhelming defeat of the military forces of the Arab states in their June 1967 war with Israel. Terrorism was by no means new to the Middle East, as Philip Windsor makes clear. But there is no doubt that as a result of this setback and the Israeli occupation of the West Bank, Gaza and the Sinai peninsula, and the Israeli takeover of the whole of Jerusalem, Palestinian militants concluded that the routes of defeating Israel by conventional military force, or regaining their homeland by diplomatic negotiation, were blocked to them. The Arab states were too divided and Israel was too militarily powerful. The militant Palestinians concluded that they would gain more by a campaign of political violence striking at Israel and its supporters internationally in a war of terrorist attrition. From 1968 to 1972 there was a tremendous upsurge of hijack attempts, bombings, shootings and other terrorist attacks against Israeli targets both in Israel and abroad, and against the airlines facilities and personnel of the United States and other Western powers that were seen in Palestinian eyes to be guilty of supporting and collaborating with Israel. This shift to terrorism was intensified after the disastrous defeat of the *fedayeen* at the hands of Hussein's forces in Jordan in autumn 1970. Between 1967 and 1974, estimates suggest that about 15 per cent of all international terrorist incidents were carried out by Palestinian groups, many of them spilling over into Western Europe.

The impact of Palestinian terrorism should not be assessed purely in quantitative terms. Reports of the actions of Palestinian terrorists, and the huge international publicity they achieved, undoubtedly interested militant groups in other parts of the world in exploiting the techniques of international terror. And we should not neglect the direct influence of the PFLP, el-Fatah and other Palestinian organizations through their work of training foreign terrorists in various camps in the Middle East and in the constant Palestinian contacts with other terrorist groups around the world.

The second development was the resurgence of the neo-Marxist and Trotskyist left among the student populations of the industrial countries. Their common rallying-points were bitter opposition to US policy in the Vietnam war, and to American policy in the Third World generally, which they designated neo-imperialism. Although the majority of the student left abandoned political violence following the street demonstrations and battles with the police in 1968–9, there remained a hard core of ideological extremists who decided that what was really needed was a more professional and long-term campaign of urban violence against the 'system'. These groups resolved to form an 'underground', which engaged in a sustained campaign of terrorism. The main groups that sprang from this movement included the Baader-Meinhof gang in the Federal Republic of Germany, the Red Brigades in Italy and the Japanese Red Army. With their shared neo-Marxist ideology and self-perceptions as part of a broader international revolutionary movement, they maintained international links with movements abroad, including the Palestinians. There is considerable evidence that they learned from each other.

Trends in modern international terrorism

The best known of the data-bases for incidents of international terrorism in the 1960s and 1970s are the Rand chronology (which tends to concentrate on the more significant or major incidents and provides fuller detail on these than the other chronologies), Edward Mickolus's ITERATE (International Terrorism: Attributes of Terrorist Events) computer system, and the Central Intelligence Agency's published statistics on international terrorism. The CIA's figures for the 1960s are, by general agreement, a considerable underestimate. Their research report for 1979 admits the unavoidably arbitrary nature of the recording procedures.[5] They deliberately excluded, for example, 'the assassinations and cross-border operations associated with the Arab-Israeli conflict, unless those incidents either victimized non-combatant nationals of states outside the principal area of conflict or became the object of international controversy'. This means that international terrorist incidents in the Middle East are considerably underreported. However, in 1980, the CIA entirely revised its figures for previous years. The reasons given were (1) that the range of data sources they had previously used was too narrow, and (2) that they had now decided to include statistics on 'threats' and 'hoaxes'. Needless to say, this led to a dramatic upward revision of the figures. The CIA's 1980 report claimed that there had been 6,714 international terrorist incidents from 1968 to 1980, whereas their 1979 report total is only 3,336.

The US Department of State has avoided some of these pitfalls of recording statistics in its own research on international terrorist incidents and published reports in the 1980s. It uses a very simple and widely accepted definition of terrorism: 'premeditated, politically motivated violence perpetrated against noncombatant targets by subnational groups or clandestine state agents, usually intended to influence an audience'. 'International' is defined as involving 'citizens or territory of more than one country'. The Department of State's statistics provide, by general agreement of the academic specialists in terrorism, the most comprehensive and accurate figures on incidents involving US targets and victimizing US citizens and property. These statistics will be used as the main source of US-related international terrorism in this paper.

As Table 4.1 shows, the figures produced by the best-known data-bases on international terrorism vary considerably. This is due mainly to differences in definition and categorization—as regards what constitutes not only an act of terrorism, but also an 'incident'. For example, Rand's chronology[6] treated a wave of 40 bombings in the same city in the same night as a single incident, whereas the CIA's data-base dealt with it as 40 separate incidents.[7] There are other major problems of erroneous information, conflicting reports from different and even from the same sources, and deliberate suppression or underreporting of information by the authorities. Nevertheless, the data-bases for the 1960s and 1970s compared in Table 4.1 are at least attempting to deal with the same universe of terrorist events. Even allowing for the differences in the counting systems used, leading to different annual totals, it is interesting that these data-bases all reflect similar broad trends in the incidence of international terrorism: a sharp rise from 1968 to 1970, followed by a brief downturn in 1971; a sharp rise in 1973; a slight drop in 1975, followed by a sharp rise in 1976.

Total confusion arises when attempts are made to analyse international terrorism on the basis of statistics derived from a data-base which mixes internal (i.e. domestic) and international terrorist incidents, especially since the international are a small proportion of all terrorist incidents. The data of Risks International, Inc., fall into this category. It is easy to see how reliance on such figures can skew perception of international terrorist trends if we examine the case of the United States. The United States has had no major indigenous political terrorist campaign. Almost all the attacks, deaths and injuries suffered by US targets since 1968 have been abroad. And, according to FBI figures, in the whole period 1980–5 only 17 people have been killed and 63 injured in terrorist attacks within United

States territory. Obviously, as a proportion of total worldwide internal *and* international terrorism, the US share is tiny.

Here, too, there is a problem with the data. The geographical location of incidents is fairly reliably recorded, even allowing for differences in definitions (Table 4.2). But there is no comprehensive cross-national data-base on the nationality of targets, only a selection of national sources. The American data on targets of international terrorist attacks in the 1970s (Table 4.3) show that US citizens or property were targeted in over 40 per cent of the total incidents worldwide. Indeed in some years—from 1969 to 1972—more than half the international incidents involved US targets and victims. In 1973, a sixth of all those who died in international attacks were Americans. In 1983, 266 Americans died through acts of international terrorism, more than had been lost in the entire preceding fifteen years of this type of violence. In a single attack on the US Marine barracks in Beirut on 23 October, the United States lost almost as many servicemen as Britain lost in the entire Falklands campaign. It is this long experience of high vulnerability to international terrorist attacks abroad which helps to explain the salience which successive US governments have given to international measures against terrorism (Table 4.4). Moreover, the highest incidence of aircraft hijacking also occurred against flights originating in the USA between 1969 and 1972. There were no fewer than 58 attempts at hijacking planes from the United States in 1971–2, although not all were politically motivated.

Nor is it merely a question of the arithmetic of atrocity. The American public and successive US administrations have been shocked, as we all have, by the dramatic and ruthless nature of particular events, powerfully relayed by the news media. An Australian scholar has pointed out that statistics on the overall level of incidents in 1975 showed a brief drop in the level of international terrorism.[8] Yet in the eyes of the media and the public it became known as 'the year of the terrorist' because of the impact of certain dramatic incidents, such as the seizure of the OPEC oil ministers in Vienna, the seizure of embassies in Stockholm, Kuala Lumpur and Madrid, and the hijacking of a train in the Netherlands.

If one compares the vulnerability to international terrorism of other countries, one finds, not surprisingly, a large number of incidents directed at Israeli targets. Israeli figures record 552 internationally derived attacks between July 1968 and March 1986, killing 490 and injuring 1,536.[9] Among the countries whose diplomats have been the most frequently targeted are the Soviet Union, the United Kingdom, Cuba, Turkey and Jordan.[10]

Data concerning the tactics of international terrorism show that explosive and incendiary bombings, shooting attacks and assassinations remain the most popular methods. All involve minimum risk of capture and punishment for the perpetrator. The popularity of other methods has fluctuated. A rash of letter-bombings in the early 1970s was ended by the introduction of automatic letter-bomb detection devices. Aircraft hijackings declined sharply after 1973, following the new stringent boarding-gate search procedures pioneered by the USA, only to increase again when terrorists learned new ways of evading airport security measures. There was a wave of embassy seizures and hostage-takings between 1979 and 1980, perhaps encouraged by the dramatic publicity achieved by the 1979 abduction of the US diplomatic mission in Tehran. But this craze declined rapidly in the face of more determined countermeasures by governments, such as the use of the SAS to end the siege at the Iranian embassy in London in May 1980.

One of the most worrying current trends is the growing lethality of attacks. In the early 1970s over 80 per cent of terrorist attacks were against buildings and other material objects. In the past five years roughly 50 per cent of international terrorist attacks have targeted people. Incidents causing deaths have increased by about 20 per cent per year, and large-scale destructive attacks, such as the truck and car bombings in Lebanon, have increased. Some of this increase in lethality is due to the ability of terrorists to make more powerful bombs. Part is probably due to the desire to achieve greater propaganda of atrocity. It is also partly explained by the appearance of a new and more fanatically ruthless generation of terrorists in certain highly active groups.

The most important trend in international terrorism is the growing significance of the Middle East as a source of terrorist violence. In 1984, as Figure 4.1 shows, 34.2 per cent of all international terrorist incidents occurred in the Middle East, and Department of State data record that in 1985 no less than 45 per cent occurred in that region. Research on this data at Aberdeen University and Rand suggests that a high proportion of these attacks (over 25 per cent) was linked in some degree to the activities of state sponsors of terrorism, their agents and secret services. It should be stressed, however, that this sponsorship varies enormously from case to case, ranging from the direct recruitment, arming and control of hit-squads, to training, assistance with cash or weapons, to mere diplomatic and propaganda support. Nor should one exaggerate the importance of financial help given by state sponsors to terrorist groups. Terrorism is comparatively cheap to organize and mount. Arab state sponsors have now far less cash available for such purposes because of plummeting oil revenues. And, as James Adams points out in an invaluable pioneering study,[11] some of the large terrorist movements have become successful capitalists, with substantial assets and investment income, and thus financially far more self-sufficient. Syria, Libya and Iran have been implicated most frequently as state sponsors. This has created special problems for the targeted states and the international community. The focus on state sponsorship, reinforced by repeated attacks on the US presence in the Middle East and the Mediterranean area, has, above all other considerations, provoked a major reappraisal of US counterterrorist policy.

International responses

At the global level, the response to international terrorism has been weak. There have been many obstacles to effective international cooperation, whether through United Nations resolutions or through other general measures. The East-West ideological conflict has resulted in mutual recrimination and accusation by the superpowers, and many states have resisted any international move which would either reduce their scope for using international terrorism as a weapon or thwart what they see as legitimate armed struggles. It is likely to be some time before the international community as a whole translates the rhetoric of recent UN resolutions against terrorism into effective enforcement measures. So far the only worthwhile general international legal achievements in this field have been the international conventions on air piracy and the protection of diplomats.

But even those Western states which have been major targets of terrorism and have an obvious common interest in combating it have been slow to agree a collective approach. None of the international organizations, even NATO, has proved an easily acceptable framework in the sensitive areas of internal security, law and order. Traditionally governments have taken the view that here they must retain sovereign control. Western politicians and judiciaries are as chauvinistic in this respect as other states, despite the many moral and legal values they have in common with fellow Western governments.

Some Western democracies have little or no direct experience of terrorism, and thus cannot see the importance of the problem. Enthusiasm for action often dissipates rapidly once shock at a specific outrage has died away. All Western governments have problems when asked to sacrifice or endanger commercial outlets, possible markets, trade links, or sources of oil or raw materials by taking really tough action against states like Libya which support terrorism. Some states fear revenge attacks from the host states, looking to placate in the hope of security. Most have double standards and condone some terrorist acts as the practice of encircled 'freedom-fighters' (e.g. the French attitude to Armenian terrorists, the Greek attitude to the Palestine Liberation Organization). Yet the need for improved international cooperation is growing. Terrorism is inherently international in character, so that, paradoxically, the more individual states improve their national measures, the more it becomes attractive for the terrorists to cross frontiers to escape justice, to secure arms, ammunition and money, and to collaborate with fellow terrorists.

The American response

The Lod airport massacre of May 1972, in which 26 passengers were killed and 76 wounded, mostly Puerto Rican pilgrims, and the Munich Olympics massacre in September of the same year, in which eleven Israeli athletes and a policeman were killed, were key factors in causing President Nixon's administration to set up the Cabinet Committee to Combat Terrorism in September 1972. If this could happen to Puerto Ricans and Israelis, then the potential threat to American citizens and interests abroad was clearly tremendous. The Committee was chaired by the Secretary of State and included the Secretaries of Defense, the Treasury and Transportation, the Attorney General, the Directors of the CIA and FBI, and the Ambassador to the UN. The Committee's only significant early effort was the attempt to obtain a new draft UN convention to suppress terrorism. This was an ambitious attempt, aimed at prevention, deterrence and punishment of crimes of international terrorism, and it failed to get agreement from the UN General Assembly because of the deep divisions among member states over the definition of terrorism.

Nevertheless, the move marked the beginning of a long series of US government initiatives to formulate and strengthen international conventions and treaties covering every aspect of the control of international terrorism, from aircraft hijacking to the prevention of hostage-taking. One of the most imaginative and successful of these initiatives was the 1973 hijack pact with Cuba. A US government working-group was also set up, consisting of senior members of the Cabinet Committee. And, in 1976, the Department of State established the Office for Combatting Terrorism to provide expert assistance and an 'operational focus for crisis management' when dealing with international terrorist incidents. It was during President Carter's administration that the Nixon Cabinet Committee was abolished and replaced by the Special Coordination Committee (SCC) of the National Security Council. These developments demonstrate the continuity of concern about international terrorism on the part of the United States, although the problem was still seen primarily in humanitarian and law-and-order terms.

Throughout the period 1968–80, US citizens and facilities were major targets of attack. But it was the abduction of the entire US diplomatic mission by Khomeini's students in Tehran in 1979 that really brought home to the American people and government that international terrorism was potentially far more than a law-and-order problem. It became identified as a major national security issue. Slogan-chanting Iranian students were able to do untold psychological damage to America's morale and international credibility—particularly in the Middle East—by maintaining their defiance of international law for months on end. As it became evident in the atmosphere of post-Vietnam trauma that the Carter administration was powerless to secure the release of the hostages, and especially after the failure of the military rescue mission, the hostage crisis became a millstone around President Carter's neck. It contributed to an image of weakness which undoubtedly played a major part in enabling Ronald Reagan to defeat Jimmy Carter in the November 1980 election. Not for the first time the public was heartily sick of seeing Americans 'pushed around' by a third-rate power, and Reagan's campaign was able to exploit this longing for an assertive foreign policy.

However harshly historians may judge the Carter administration's overall handling of the hostage crisis, they will at least give it some credit for successfully concluding the complex diplomatic negotiations which brought the hostages' release in 1981. But, in the shadow of this traumatic experience, in view of the Reagan camp's profound commitment to opposing communist expansion in all its forms and given its belief that international terrorism was communist-inspired, it was hardly surprising that the new administration started out by declaring that combating international terrorism was one of its major priorities. The urgency with which President Reagan and the new Secretary of State, Alexander Haig, pursued this aim was increased by two further factors: (1) their belief that the Soviet Union was the author of a major international conspiracy to use terrorism to undermine the free world, and (2) their determination to defeat what they saw as the direct threat to US security from the subversion and terrorism exported by the revolutionary regimes in Cuba and Nicaragua in their own hemisphere. With apparently perfect timing, an American journalist published a book which dramatically suggested that the Soviet Union and its allies were behind *The Terror Network*, while the State Department produced a whole dossier of alleged evidence to establish the substantial assistance given by Cuba and Nicaragua to Marxist guerrilla forces in El Salvador.[12]

This conjunction of events served not only to place the problem of combating international terrorism much higher on the American policy agenda, but to increase public awareness and concern. Unfortunately, it also had the effect of vastly oversimplifying the debate. International terrorism became a fashionable 'boo' word for any movement or foreign intervention seen as inimical to American interests, often a mere synonym for attempts at communist revolution. Concentration on the alleged Soviet role tended to blind many observers to the hydra-headed and complex nature of terrorist violence across the world. The picture was distorted in that it obscured the deep indigenous roots of many groups using terrorist methods, and the complex variety of ideologies, political aims and state sponsors involved.

Whereas the debate on terrorism in the first Reagan administration was marked by mounting confusion about definition and causes, since October 1983 attention has increasingly centred on the so-called military options for dealing with international terrorist attacks against Americans and on how to hit back at the alleged state sponsors of such attacks. This new focus to the policy debate, still very much alive in Washington, emerged in reaction to the massacre of US Marines and French troops on 23 October 1983 by Shi'ite terrorists using truck bombs. Whatever the merits of the case for American involvement in Lebanon (an issue hotly debated inside the USA as well as elsewhere), this attack was more lethal than any in the history of modern international terrorism: the United States lost more lives in Lebanon in 1983 than it had in the preceding fifteen years of international terrorist incidents. But what caused the intense policy debate in Washington was not simply the scale of the attack and the weaknesses in security that it exposed (though these were inevitably major issues), but the realization that the terrorists had succeeded in forcing the US government to plan the withdrawal of the US Marines from Lebanon, thereby limiting US policy options in the Middle East. In brutal terms, it demonstrated that terrorism was a potent weapon even against the military and economic might of a superpower.

The propaganda of atrocity reached its target in the US media, public and Congress, and created pressures for policy changes which the President and his advisers were quite unable to withstand. They feared that other factions, and the states which Washington suspected of sponsoring the attacks on Americans in Beirut, would seek to emulate the Shi'ite attacks. Hence the urgency with which President Reagan, near the end of his first term, signed a new National Security Decision Directive ordering the government to explore and develop the military options to deal with international terrorism. Secretary of State George Schultz made a speech on 3 April 1984, the same day that the President signed the new directive, stating that if the nation were to combat state-sponsored international terrorism successfully, America must be prepared to use force. Since that date there has been growing evidence of a divergence of views within the administration concerning the circumstances under which the use of force would be appropriate and the ways in which such force should be used.

Now that the US government has used military force in a reprisal action against Libya, there must always be the possibility that it will decide on similar action again, either against the Gaddafi regime or against some other state sponsor if occasion demands. There is a sense in which major powers and their leaders become prisoners of their own rhetoric. Having justified each action so strongly in the Libyan case, the administration might find it difficult to resist the pressures for the use of force on a future occasion.

American policy-makers have been deeply frustrated by West European backsliding, as it appears to them, especially in relation to Libya, all the more so because the statistics demonstrate the continuing vulnerability of Western Europe to international terrorist incidents.[13] Britain and the Federal Republic of Germany have been largely exempted from the criticisms, and of course Mrs Thatcher's willingness to allow US F-111 planes to fly from British bases further enhanced the British reputation in Washington. But several other European governments have been roundly criticized for their placatory attitudes, especially the French, Greek, Italian and Spanish. West Europeans have seriously underestimated the strength of feeling in the United States. For example, Americans have been angered by the attitude of successive French governments in sanctioning deals behind the scenes with several international terrorist groups, including Armenians and the Abu Nidal group, in efforts to stave off further attacks on French territory. The US government believes that the principle 'France, terre d'asile' has been elevated to a sacred cow and prevents the extradition of persons wanted for questioning about terrorist offences. The Italian authorities' handling of the *Achille Lauro* hijack only served to confirm American frustration with West European attitudes.

West European reluctance to introduce economic sanctions against Libya following the Vienna and Rome airport outrages of December 1985 further fuelled American anger, though the US government saw the declaration at the Tokyo summit of May 1986 as a welcome sign of progress.[14] (There is a certain irony in the fact that the US government has echoed Mrs Thatcher in taking a strong line against the use of economic sanctions against South Africa: yet another example of the inconsistency of US foreign policy under Reagan.) Nevertheless, the US government, as well as much American opinion, sees the West Europeans' unreadiness to sacrifice any of the lucrative contracts and economic links that they have developed with Tripoli, and their criticism of the US bombing raids on Libya, as still more evidence that its allies are not willing to help the United States against any enemy other than the Soviet Union.

Meanwhile, in America, the President is still basking in considerable popularity for having been seen at last to have 'done something' about terrorism. It is this very domestic political success of the raid, in President Reagan's terms, that should alert West European leaders to the need to put together an effective transatlantic policy on dealing with state-sponsored terrorism. There is little doubt that further unilateral military reprisals or 'pre-emptive' strikes by the United States would deepen the divisions in the North Atlantic Alliance, encouraging still further the Americanization of America and the Europeanization of Europe.

Other essays in this volume address the broader implications of terrorism for international order, but the following general points on trends in Western responses need to be made. (1) There is no evidence that military reprisals actually stop or reduce terrorism, and this is admitted by the American government. (2) If military reprisals or 'pre-emptive strikes' are undertaken in certain circumstances, they may result in an escalation to an international war which is more dangerous and destructive of life and property than the terrorism one is supposedly eradicating. (This is what happened as a result of Israel's war against terrorism in Lebanon in 1982.) (3) There is some historical evidence that legal, diplomatic, political and economic actions vis-à-vis regimes violating international norms do at least isolate, and can politically weaken, those regimes. (4) Finally, even though legal, diplomatic, political and economic actions are by no means a proven panacea for eliminating state-sponsored terrorism and the terrorism of non-state actors, if *concerted* they could substantially *reduce* international terrorism. At least they do not carry the risk of international war.

Notes

1. See, for example, Claire Sterling, *The Terror Network* (London, Weidenfeld & Nicolson, 1981), and Benjamin Netanyahu (ed.), *Terrorism: How the West Can Win* (London, Weidenfeld & Nicolson, 1986).
2. There is an impressive array of evidence for the 'common ground' among scholars in Alex P. Schmid, *Political Terrorism: A Research Guide to Concepts, Theories, Data Bases and Literature* (Amsterdam, North Holland Publishing Company, 1983), pp. 5–159. For early discussions of the definitional problem, see Paul Wilkinson, 'Three

Questions on Terrorism', *Government and Opposition*, vol. 8 (1973), no.3, pp. 290–312, and at greater length the same author's *Political Terrorism* (London, Macmillan, 1974).

3. For fuller discussions of typology, see Schmid, *Political Terrorism*; Paul Wilkinson, *Terrorism and the Liberal State*, 2nd edn (London, Macmillan, 1986), pp. 23–33; and Eugene V. Walter, *Terror and Resistance: A Study of Political Violence* (London, Oxford University Press, 1969), pp. 3–27.

4. The nature and *modus operandi* of state-sponsored international terrorism is discussed in Wilkinson, *Terrorism and the Liberal State*, ch. 16. For a historical study of the Soviet role, see Galia Golan, *The Soviet Union and the PLO*, Adelphi Paper No. 131 (London, International Institute for Strategic Studies, 1976).

5. *International Terrorism in 1979: A Research Paper* (US National Foreign Assessment Center, Washington, DC, 1980), Appendix A, 'Interpreting Statistics on International Terrorism'.

6. Brian Jenkins and Janera Johnson, *International Terrorism: A Chronology*, Rand Publication Series, Report No. R-1597-DOS-ARPA, March 1975, and supplement, R-1909-1-ARPA, February 1976 (Rand Corporation, Santa Monica, CA).

7. This is noted in *International Terrorism in 1979*, Appendix A.

8. Grant Wardlaw, *Political Terrorism* (Cambridge, Cambridge University Press, 1982), p. 51.

9. Israeli Defence Forces report, cited in *Maariv*, 17 April 1986.

10. *Terrorist Attacks Against Diplomats: A Statistical Overview of International Terrorist Attacks on Diplomatic Personnel and Facilities from January 1968 to June 1981* (Department of State, Washington, DC, 1981).

11. James Adams, *The Financing of Terror* (London, New English Library, 1986).

12. Parts of this dossier were reproduced in *The Soviet-Cuban Connection in Central America and the Caribbean* (Department of State and Department of Defense, Washington, DC, March 1985).

13. *Patterns of Global Terrorism, 1984* (Department of State, Washington, DC, 1985), p. ii.

14. For a fuller discussion of the summit agreement and its weaknesses, see Paul Wilkinson, 'Gemeinsam gegen die Gewalt', *Die Zeit*, No. 24, 6 June 1986.

5

Terrorism and strategy

LAWRENCE FREEDMAN

My objective in this paper is to consider terrorism as a problem in
military strategy. This requires considering both terrorism and
counterterrorism as a strategy, and that in turn requires a degree of
analysis of the concept of terrorism itself.

The classification of acts as being 'terroristic' is in no sense
precise. Terrorism is distinct from other military strategies, not in
exploiting violence or the threat of violence in pursuit of political
objectives, but in playing on the psychology of violence. It works,
not through brute force, but through the fear aroused in potential
victims, especially those not professionally trained to cope with
violence. There is an inevitable tendency to reserve the label not so
much for the methods as for the purposes: 'terrorism' conveys a
sense of illegitimacy. To label a group terrorist can constitute an
ideological victory. Meanwhile other groups that employ similar
methods are excused because of the justice of their cause. Thus the
Contras in Nicaragua, or the rebel groups in Afghanistan, might be
considered freedom-fighters in the West, while to their victims they
appear less wholesome.

However, a discussion of terrorism in strategic terms requires a
broad definition. The methods of terrorism are not the monopoly of
any cause or political philosophy. During World War II, partisan
groups in occupied territory employed on occasion such methods,
for example against collaborators or informers. The African

National Congress in South Africa now does the same. Nor are these methods the monopoly of non-governmental groups. The South African response to ANC activity in neighbouring countries, and the US response to Libya's sponsoring of terrorism, may involve similar techniques. The fact that the former was condemned by the British government, and the latter supported, indicates the need to employ a definition of terrorism and counterterrorism that is as politically neutral as possible.

This does not mean that we can ignore questions of legitimacy when considering terrorism, for terrorism must be assessed by reference to the overall political and military circumstances in which it is practised. Although it is often used most effectively against individuals who, while not necessarily in uniform, are nevertheless closely associated with the governing regime, it attracts most opprobrium when it deliberately puts non-combatants at risk. Such violence is deemed, at worst, to be irretrievably criminal rather than politico-military, and at best it is recognized to require special justification. Thus, for instance, a distinction can be made between actions that are directed against repressive regimes, a category that effectively rules out more peaceful, alternative forms of pressure, and actions taken in those democratic countries where peaceful means of persuasion are available. Such arguments have been used, for example, to explain why the IRA should be denounced and the ANC supported.

The need for special justification indicates the extent to which terrorism appears, along with political violence of all types, to reflect a sense of desperation rather than a calculation of the optimum method for achieving goals. In democratic societies, only objectives that are hopelessly extreme force their proponents to desperate strategies. Elsewhere there may be a lack of suitable means to obtain quite modest objectives. Adoption of extreme goals, or lack of alternative means, or a combination of the two, can result in terrorism.

Terrorism: strategic and tactical

It is therefore important to take terrorism seriously as a strategy and not just to regard it as an outrage. Military strategy is concerned with the employment of military means to achieve political objectives. Anyone contemplating being on the receiving end of military force is liable to feel a degree of terror at the prospect, and this might be expected to influence behaviour. The response can take a variety of forms. With an individual soldier it might lead to a surge of adrenalin or an exploration of opportunities for desertion. For a civilian population it might take the form of stoic resistance or panic.

If terrorism is to be effective strategically, it must be able to generate a particular response. The response will depend upon such factors as the victim's sense of vulnerability to the threat, the degree of protection and the extent of countermeasures available, as well as the moral claims and legitimacy of those responsible for the terror. It will also relate to whether there are political responses that might remove or reduce the threat. A strategy of terrorism is therefore one which seeks to influence an adversary's behaviour through the threat of the hurt that will be faced should he not comply with political demands. Actual violence is not necessarily part of the strategy. It might be hoped, for example, that the mere threat of a bombing campaign will produce the desired results without it being necessary to cause anyone any hurt. If need be, to drive the point home, a few well-placed and well-timed explosions can be used to emphasize the vulnerability of potential victims. The recent campaign waged by the Basque separatist organization, ETA, against the Spanish tourist industry comes into this category. What is most distinctive about *strategic* terrorism is its *primary* reliance on terror to achieve objectives—the belief that such methods can be decisive in themselves. It is worth distinguishing this from what might be called *tactical* terrorism, which is in practice more frequent. Here terrorism is employed as one of several instruments in pursuit of a broader strategy.

As a strategy, therefore, terrorism must be purposive. The purposes are not always easy to discern because of the nature of terrorism—and terrorists—but it must be distinguished from pathological violence. So, for example, the assassin of a political leader may have a severe personality disorder, a grudge against the leader as an individual, a fantasy about acquiring a place in the history books, or a belief that as a result of this assassination important political changes will take place. It is only the last factor that would give the act a strategic quality. It may of course be bad strategy, not only in ethical terms but in terms of achieving the desired results, and the inadequacy of the underlying analysis. It may be verging on the irrational, in that there is only the most tenuous relationship between the means employed and the desired ends. It may be self-consciously an act of desperation. Nonetheless this would be strategic as opposed to pathological terrorism. There is a long but by no means distinguished history of political strategies—varieties of anarchism, such as nihilism and Blanquism—based on such dubious judgments yet adopted by otherwise intelligent people. More recent versions are the Angry Brigade in Britain, the Weathermen in the United States and the Baader-Meinhof gang in Germany, which grew out of the student protest movement of the late 1960s and represent a combination of extreme ideology with political immaturity.

Equally, acts that are purposive and put non-combatants at risk are not necessarily terroristic. For example, airliners may be hijacked in order to reach a particular destination. Although this may be very frightening for the other passengers, the act would be strategic only if the hijacked passengers were then used as hostages to exact some political price. Blackmail and extortion depend on fear, but the objective may be no more than personal gain. Much terrorist activity is in practice devoted to goals largely related to sustaining the groups themselves—using kidnapping to gain funds or hijacks to obtain the release of imprisoned comrades—rather than promoting the long-term goals that supposedly motivate them. Bank robberies and kidnappings in the Irish Republic may have been undertaken to support terrorism, but in practice they are often indistinguishable from other types of criminal activity.

A variety of military strategies are in essence terroristic, and not just those that are normally distinguished by the name. The blitz of British cities and the subsequent allied bombing of Germany were criticized, apart from anything else, for a readiness to take human life in the hope that this would affect the 'morale' of factory workers, or for some other ill-defined strategic objective. These strategies were also to some extent embarked upon in the absence of more effective ways of getting at the enemy, and were bitterly criticized by the victims as being beyond the bounds of civilized conduct. In one of his most famous phrases, Sir Winston Churchill described how, through nuclear deterrence, 'peace would become the sturdy child of terror'. The very idea of a 'balance of terror' recognizes that nuclear weapons gain their effects through the fear of their employment. Much nuclear strategy is concerned with the manipulation of threats. There is of course a difference in that governments rarely depend wholly on such methods: at worst the terrorism is *tactical*; or, if it is *strategic*, as in the nuclear area, the aim is largely to deter comparable acts by the other side. Although such acts may still need special justification, the problems of legitimacy may be less pressing. Nonetheless, to appreciate the strategic issues raised by terrorism, we need to recognize the links with more familiar and legitimate forms of military strategy.

The connection becomes much clearer when one considers the extent to which strategies of guerrilla warfare, and indeed some of counter-insurgency, employ terroristic tactics. This is important in that many of those indulging in strategic terrorism would be tactical terrorists if it were possible to employ terror on a more local and focused basis, and in conjunction with other tactics and political initiatives. IRA terrorism within Northern Ireland, for example, is more tactical than IRA campaigns in mainland Britain, which are more strategic in character.

Direct control and indirect influence

Strategic terror is likely to flourish in particular conditions, which can best be identified in terms of the objectives of those who are employing the terror. Here a distinction belonging to the objectives of military strategy in general is helpful: namely, that between the objectives of *direct control* and *indirect influence*. Traditionally, military strategy aims at *direct control*: that is, to obtain or secure a piece of territory or to take over the government. It requires physical occupation of the relevant territory, or political centres, or whatever is in dispute. There is, in a sense, a transfer of political power.

Indirect influence is very much second best. It does not involve a transfer of effective power, but instead affects the circumstances in which that power is exercised. Because it is indirect, there is not necessarily a sense of *force majeure*. If the enemy is prepared to accept whatever the costs and inconveniences may be, he can still resist responding to the demands made upon him. Traditional military options are geared to direct control (following a defeat of enemy forces in battle). Resort to strategies of indirect influence implies a lack of such options.

Terrorism may be employed tactically in pursuit of either direct control or indirect influence. For example, insurgents with a long-term objective of overthrowing a particular government or obtaining regional autonomy may start with terroristic acts but with the hope of being able to take on the regular forces of the state in more traditional combat. They would judge that early terrorism directed against the forces of the state would lead to their demoralization, while the mere fact of taking on the authorities would in some way gain popular respect and practical support. This is the idea of the *foco*, or revolutionary cell, as developed in the writings of the theorists of the Cuban revolution, such as Che Guevara and Régis Debray, and unsuccessfully applied later in Bolivia.

Terrorism is likely to be most prominent as part of a strategy of indirect influence in situations in which alternative options have been ruled out. Such strategies unavoidably have to rely on threats and intimidation. So strategies of indirect influence are very much second best to direct control, which indicates that the methods of terrorism are by and large also second best to more traditional military methods.

In order to exert indirect influence effectively, the following conditions must be met. It must be made clear to those who are to be influenced what is expected of them. They must have the power to do what is expected. The costs of not implementing these demands must exceed the costs of implementing them. Those making the demands must therefore threaten severe punishment and be convincing in their threats.

Conditions for effectiveness

It is extraordinarily rare for terrorist action to meet these requirements, for it does not lend itself to fine-tuning military means to political ends. This can be seen if one examines some of the issues faced by those employing terrorism. These issues are relevant both for situations involving non-governmental groups (groups seeking to overthrow or influence governments) and for situations in which terroristic methods have been adopted by a government. Because the latter case raises special issues, for the moment we will concentrate on non-governmental groups. Three distinctions are of interest: discriminate/indiscriminate; overt/ covert; national/transnational.

Discriminate/indiscriminate

Terrorists may well insist that they are being discriminatory, that they are after 'legitimate military or political targets', and that any associated civilian casualties are unfortunate but the 'sort of thing that happens in war'—what in military jargon would be known as 'collateral damage'. Their objective is to terrorize the 'state apparatus' itself or, say, the 'agents of colonialism'. However, because they find it difficult to isolate their 'legitimate' targets and because their competence and capabilities are not always sufficient, targets are often attacked with substantial collateral damage, or indeed missed altogether and only the innocent hurt. Moreover, this may be a consequence of acts that have only property as their targets and do not seek to harm people at all.

For those fighting among their own people, as part of a strategy of direct control, discrimination in practice, rather than simply intention, is extremely important. They are dependent on local support, in terms of food, shelter, manpower, funds and political sympathy, and cannot afford to alienate this support by inflicting tragedy upon them. In these circumstances, if used at all, terror is most effective when used 'tactically' and against targets generally recognized to be legitimate. A group vulnerable to exposure to the authorities will seek to terrorize potential informers. However, those operating away from home are likely to be both less able and less willing to be discriminate. They may well be more disposed to accept that they can get at the enemy only through his civilian population. They do not expect to be liked; it is more important that they be feared. This encourages strategic terror.

Overt/covert

The question of overt/covert relates to the ability of the terrorists to claim credit (or accept blame) for their actions. An act of terrorism depends on stealth and effective cover. At issue is the link between the act itself and a known political entity. It is notable that, unlike criminal acts, there is rarely a shortage of volunteers coming

forward to claim credit for acts of terrorism. The same acts are often
claimed by quite different groups. So, as a strategy, terrorism
depends on a clear relationship being established between a pattern
of activity and a political programme. Since, especially in this media
age, terrorist activity can serve as a means of gaining attention, it is
vital to be able to exploit this attention by giving interviews, issuing
manifestos and generally gaining political credibility. The objective
of direct control is unlikely to be attained while a group is forced to
stay underground and is confined to covert activity.

To come out into the open, however, is to provide intelligence
with regard to the individuals involved and their location, which
might be vital to the enemy. So a truly overt approach may be too
dangerous. It may be possible to rely on sympathizers who, while
keeping their distance from the terrorists themselves, will nonetheless seek to exploit publicity to promote the cause (for instance, by
blaming the violence on the authorities for not giving in to a set of
demands). In Ireland, although the IRA is a banned organization,
its political wing, Sinn Fein, is not, and this allows for a sustained
political presence. It can of course also create tensions between the
political and military wings if, for example, the politicians start to
feel that military activities are becoming a hindrance rather than a
help. Even terrorist groups can have problems with political control!

Generally, in order to maintain a political presence, terrorist
groups need a 'safe' area of some sort, either a region that has come
to be effectively under control or a sanctuary in another country.
Groups that take credit for terrorist acts merely by phoning a news
agency or delivering a letter, with impressive names that imply great
support (using words like 'Popular', 'Front', 'People's', etc.), but
without any obvious political base, are unlikely to convince either
adversaries or potential supporters that they are a force to be
reckoned with. It is important to remember that terrorist acts gain
political credibility through the prospect of repetition and the
consequent sense of irresistibility. Such power and continuity is
impossible to develop without an overt political presence as well as a
covert military presence.

It must be noted that, whatever the rhetoric, governments do on
occasion talk to those whom they have labelled 'terrorist' or who
have failed to renounce violence as a means of political change.
When it came to granting independence to colonies, British governments often found themselves negotiating with leaders who were

associated with violent protest—for example, Kenyatta in Kenya, who had been linked by the British with Mau-Mau. In the early 1970s there were even some talks with the IRA. More recently it has been found expedient to establish contact with the PLO and ANC. The point is that these groups commanded attention, despite their readiness to adopt violent tactics, because of their degree of popular support.

Transnational/national

Finally, the transnational/national distinction refers to whether or not the terrorist group is able to base itself effectively in the country (or set of countries) whose political structure it most seeks to affect, or whether it must rely on an external base. If a group is aiming at direct control rather than indirect influence, it must seek to operate nationally. This does not preclude an additional transnational level of activity, especially if the objective is to expose the enemy's international vulnerabilities. The utility of international airlines for those seeking to make a dramatic and violent political point has attracted the notice of many groups who are also able to operate within their own country—for example, the radical Sikhs in India.

There are of course some groups that seek to operate transnationally because they have a transnational cause or ideology. Their activity may be linked to another country in which that ideology reigns supreme. Cases of this sort will be discussed later. There are also cases where the groups are based on a dispersed ethnic entity— Armenians, Kurds, Palestinians. Lastly, disparate groups that share some ideological precepts may find it convenient to keep in touch and help each other. They may unite in a common cause—for example, support of the PLO. In Europe in the 1980s there has been a coordinated campaign against a variety of NATO targets that reflects links of this sort.

Governments fighting for direct control against a violent opposition will seek to deny their opponents a secure national base and, if possible, sanctuary in neighbouring countries. Groups forced to operate transnationally will find it difficult to develop and draw upon their political constituency. Unless they can do this, their strategies will inevitably be those of indirect influence.

It may be difficult to operate effectively inside the enemy territory at all, as has been the experience of Palestinian groups attempting to operate inside Israel, despite an intensive effort over many years. It has even proved difficult to attack Israeli targets overseas. Consequently, these groups have sought to exert influence extremely indirectly by attempting to shake Israel's international support.

The conclusion to be drawn from all this is that non-governmental groups are unlikely to prosper through military means if they are forced (or choose) to become indiscriminate, covert and transnational. They will certainly find it very difficult to obtain direct control, and will even find it difficult to exert indirect influence because of the problems they face in (a) sustaining a level of activity that would pressure an adversary into changing fundamental policies, (b) giving clear indications as to the changes required if the pressure is to be lifted, and (c) creating confidence that the pressure will indeed be lifted if the changes are implemented. Moreover, whereas discriminate, overt and national activity is likely to involve many elements, of which only a small proportion depend on terror, indiscriminate, covert and transnational activity tends to depend on what most people would consider to be quintessentially terroristic methods and comes under our heading of strategic terror.

All this suggests that *dependence* on terrorism is often a sign of strategic failure. What are frequently described as 'victories for terrorism' may be policy changes that have been taken for other reasons; or else, when such changes have in fact been achieved in direct response to terrorism, they tend to be for purposes of publicity or the release of other terrorists. In other words, at most they help to sustain the terrorist campaign (by gaining release of prisoners, funds to support future operations, a degree of notoriety) but are unlikely ever to be sufficient to bring the campaign to a successful conclusion.

There are three important qualifications to be made here. The first is that a 'successful' terrorist operation, defined in narrow operational terms, may be geared more to a power struggle *within* a broad political movement than to achieving much response from those whom the movement as a whole may oppose. The second is that if an act triggers an inappropriate or disproportionate response from the adversary, then that might provide a political opportunity. A brutal response may be exactly what is wanted: the worst thing for a terrorist is to be ignored. Third, whereas it may be difficult to obtain positive political goals by these methods, negative ones are easier to achieve. Terrorist acts can perform a wrecking function—by raising

the political temperature, provoking countermeasures, and so on—
at a time when a period of calm would favour constructive
diplomacy in a direction opposed by the terrorists. This has clearly
been a pattern in the Middle East and Ireland, where terrorist acts
are often designed to interfere with 'moderate' political processes,
which require delicate diplomacy and so are easily blown off course.
This 'wrecking' can be sufficient to generate—or at least provide the
trigger for—a major international crisis. After all, World War I
started with a terrorist incident.

The successes of strategic terrorism, therefore, are largely negative. Terrorism is at its most deadly and effective when tactical: that
is, when part of a concerted campaign for direct control, enjoying a
level of popular support which is substantial even if limited by
region, ethnicity or ideology, and which is geared to the seizure of
state power or the establishment of a separate political entity.

State terrorism

Up to now we have focused largely on non-governmental terrorism.
State terrorism, by which is meant acts of terror directly sponsored
by a recognized government, tends to be covert. Acts of terror
against the nationals of other countries invite retaliation and condemnation. There has been speculation in the past as to the
involvement of the intelligence services of the major powers in a
variety of covert actions. The bulk of these do not involve the taking
of human life, but have to do with intelligence collection or non-
violent forms of subversion. When it comes to all types of subversion, most governments prefer to operate through opposition groups
in the countries being subverted rather than attempt to engage in
such activity themselves. They can provide finance, arms, training
and facilities (such as passports). On occasion the support of some
rebel group has become an accepted feature of foreign policy—for
example, the US support of the Contras in Nicaragua. However, it is
normally expedient for both the opposition groups and their
external sponsors to ensure that the links between the two receive the
minimum publicity.

The desire to keep matters covert reflects a respect of international
norms of behaviour. Countries that lack such respect, or feel
disadvantaged by the international system, may be less worried

about remaining covert. These maverick states may see their willingness to flout the norms as part of their strength. However, since such an approach carries enormous risks, it is best backed up by more substantial sources of strength.

A distinction can be drawn between covert activity directly related to the security of the state and that related to broader foreign policy goals (such as promoting the ideologically congenial or undermining the uncongenial): that in the former category is less likely to be undertaken through opposition groups. It may well take the form of action directed against those attempting to subvert one's own government who have based themselves abroad. (Much Libyan terrorism has been of this nature.) It is likely to be an extension of domestic repression: intolerance of dissidence may force opposition groups and individuals into exile, where they may be chased by government agents to prevent them organizing abroad.

Nations externalizing their internal problems in this manner may have no interest whatsoever in the countries hosting their victims, although this does not reduce the effects of the hunt-and-kill on the host country. Because of the issues raised, and some of the methods employed, this form of state terrorism merges into some types of counterterrorism and will be discussed below.

Support for subversive groups operating in other countries can be part of a strategy of direct control or indirect influence. For example, North Vietnam's support for the National Liberation Front in South Vietnam, whatever its original basis, was soon geared to taking over the South. As often as not, the support is ideological and reflects a hope that a congenial philosophy will take root in another country. It should also be recognized that subversive groups may be sponsored, not in order to promote positive objectives, but in order to destabilize a potential rival. One extreme and somewhat dated example is German support for Irish nationalists and Bolsheviks during World War I. Support of this kind, as part of a strategy of indirect influence, requires a degree of cynicism in that it may be necessary to desert the group if the objective is achieved. For example, Iranian support for the Kurds against Iraq in the mid-1970s was used to gain a deal with Iraq, after which the Kurds were abandoned.

Where a group with a pronounced ideology has seized control in a particular country, there is a tendency to seek to spread the message in neighbouring countries. Radical groups elsewhere are likely to look at such political success as an inspiration and example. This was to some extent how the Communist International operated between the wars. In the 1960s, a number of groups established themselves in Latin America seeking to emulate Castro's success in Cuba. More recently, the success of Islamic fundamentalism in Iran has led to links with would-be imitators elsewhere in the Islamic world. In these circumstances, the links may be no greater than advice and occasional aid. If the groups become dependent upon the lead state, then they risk becoming the instruments of its foreign policy. This was the fate of many communist parties in the 1920s and 1930s, and of the Syrian-supported factions of the PLO more recently.

Counterterrorism

Counterterrorist strategies can be discussed in similar terms to terrorist strategies: that is, in terms of discrimination, openness and transnationalism, and with the objectives of direct control or indirect influence in mind. By and large, counterterrorists are motivated by considerations of internal security and thus direct control.

In this sense, countering terrorism is but one aspect of what is generally termed low-intensity warfare or counter-insurgency. The literature on this area provides clear guidelines: on the importance of keeping the adversary isolated and denying him popular support; on the need to gain the support of the population by both offering protection against adversary action and providing—if necessary through political, economic and social reforms—counter-attractions to adversary blandishments. At some point, political, economic and social reform might be such as to dramatically alter the circumstances of the ruling group. In this case, what we are talking about is much more than a tactical matter and goes to the heart of the question of why the opposition groups have formed in the first place and how they can sustain themselves. It may often be that the only reforms that could truly help would involve virtual capitulation to the adversary's demands. This can be the case when what is at stake is not so much social and economic conditions but movements demanding regional autonomy. The political context is therefore crucial.

If little can be done to win over the adversary's potential sources of support, it is at least necessary that the counterterrorist strategy should not make the political position worse, for example through a clumsy and indiscriminate 'search' for terrorists, or by the seizure of dissidents who have generally acted responsibly and non-violently, or by crude measures of retaliation. Far more effective is to isolate the adversary from possible sources of support through both physical and political measures. Discrimination and political sensitivity are therefore prerequisites.

A population alienated from the authorities will provide a fertile base for opposition of all types. In military terms it is vital to keep the terrorists/rebels isolated and unable to establish a base. This explains why a challenge that is firmly rooted in a particular region is more difficult to eliminate (although, for the same reason, possibly easier to contain) than one that is more widely based. The requirement to deny the rebels a base is likely to extend to neighbouring territories. Hence the raids by Israel against the PLO bases in all neighbouring states at different times (which have largely succeeded in making it difficult for the PLO to mount effective operations inside Israel) and South Africa's raids into the 'frontline' black African states. Hence, also, Britain's anxiety to improve relations with the Republic of Ireland so as to deny the IRA safe havens across the Northern Ireland border. Spain's concern about ETA sanctuaries in France is similar. It is of note that the host country's cooperation in these matters may depend on the extent to which the terrorist group is making a nuisance of itself. As the experiences of Kampuchea and Lebanon demonstrate, a weak country unable to control a group operating from within its borders soon lays itself open to interference by that group's enemies and to further weakening itself.

There is a thin line between harbouring refugees from a neighbouring country and sponsoring an insurgency, simply because refugee camps serve as natural bases and sources of recruits for an insurgency. From Kabul's point of view, the Pakistani toleration of rebel Afghan groups is tantamount to state terrorism. However, there is clearly a difference between states like Pakistan or Thailand which, probably unwittingly, find that their border areas have been taken over by another's civil war, and those states which deliberately sponsor terrorism as an instrument of national policy. As we have already noted, much of what passes for 'state terrorism' is in fact an extension of internal repression.

Countries whose territory is being used by the agents of other countries or political groups to conduct their private quarrels may not be under direct threat, but they will see political murders on their soil as a violation of national sovereignty. At worst, if the problem becomes chronic in an unstable country, it can be an unwelcome source of additional strain. If the culprit can be positively identified, this can lead to diplomatic protests, severance of relations, and so on. Otherwise the only responses are the old stand-bys of better surveillance and keen security.

More difficult as a practical matter are those groups and individuals who feel free to roam the globe in order to attack targets related to some particular cause. Such groups and individuals are likely to reflect the internationalization of a challenge to state authority that has been met effectively and possibly ruthlessly at the national level. To say, therefore, that the problem would go away if the state in question were more responsive to the demands of these groups is true but not necessarily very useful, in that their demands may well be precisely the sort that the state would find it impossible to meet.

By its very weakness, transnational terrorism is forced to rely on the international transport system to provide targets, and on the international media to provide publicity and the communication of political demands. Success in dealing with terrorism of this sort, as has often been noted, depends on good surveillance, cooperation among intelligence agencies, and the denial of access, as far as possible, to both the transport system and the media. However, while much trivial terrorism can be handled in this way, there will always be limits to success when a group is determined and well-organized.

The backing of a state may help these groups with organization and funds, or access to the transport system by means of passports and less tightly policed airports, or opportunities to gain media attention. But state sponsorship of terrorism of this transnational and indiscriminate variety creates a clear challenge to the international community.

The response to the challenge will largely and properly be non-military. It will involve cooperation in the areas outlined above and attempts to isolate offending countries. If, however, a military response is deemed appropriate, it is unlikely to form part of a strategy of direct control, since this would be accompanied by all the problems normally associated with the occupation of another country. As Israel found in the Lebanon, occupying forces can provide choice targets for terrorism when these forces have managed to attract a high degree of local resentment.

So the relevant strategies will tend to be of indirect influence, warning the state in question of the consequences of failing to stop its unacceptable behaviour. There are two aspects to implementing such strategies. First, to take on another country in this way is itself provocative and can lead to substantial political costs. At the very least it is necessary to pin responsibility for the offences unequivocally onto the accused country, and to demonstrate that the proposed response will have the desired effect and not make things worse.

This leads on to the second aspect, which is our main concern here. We noted earlier the conditions required if a strategy of indirect influence is to succeed: clarity of political demands; a reasonable expectation that they can be met; and a credible capacity to inflict unacceptable punishment should they not be met. Because the relationship between a particular state and acts of terror abroad may be difficult to establish, there is a risk that the demands will be framed in such general terms that there will be no specific criteria by which to judge whether the offender has or has not mended his ways. Furthermore, the nature of this sort of activity is such that it may be difficult to know whether the counterterrorist action has had the desired effect. There may be a lull in visible activity and then, when the fuss has died down, it may pick up again.

Any nation with a modern air force can inflict punishment on another (although the complexity of the American strikes against Libya warns of the quality of systems required against even modest opposition). In addition, operations of this sort will be influenced by a number of factors other than straightforward military capability. These in part reflect the need to demonstrate to national and international audiences that the response is warranted and in accord with international law. Reassuring these audiences may not always be consistent with maximum effectiveness.

Economic measures will generally be mooted, and even implemented, prior to military measures. Economic sanctions will often be little more than statements of commitment, an expression of a willingness to take at least some stiff action. There is rarely confidence that they will bring the adversary to his knees. Indeed, there is widespread agreement that economic sanctions are generally ineffectual, for they are difficult to enforce and take time to bite. At best they might serve over an extended period as an instrument of indirect influence.

There are certainly reasons for caution in the use of such measures. Those required to implement economic sanctions tend to suffer loss and inconvenience as a result and, unlike the armed services, do not see their natural role to be a servant of foreign policy. The record warns of the extent to which a resourceful and broadly self-sufficient country can cope with economic pressure. Sanctions offer so many temptations for lucrative deals that it is virtually impossible to achieve economic isolation. Furthermore, although sanctions may serve as a means of making a political point without violence, if they prove to be at all effective they will cause suffering and distress to the innocent. In this respect they are less discriminatory than many forms of military action and are not a painless alternative.

However, none of this justifies the bald statement that 'sanctions never work'. Against countries with weak economies and in debt (possibly the conditions of countries supporting terrorism) they can hurt. Indeed in some instances the risk is of being *too* successful, in that if a country of any economic significance collapses, the repercussions around the international financial community will be considerable. The most vulnerable to these measures are therefore peripheral countries with no great input into the global economy yet dependent upon it. Over a period of time, the victim and the international community will both adjust to sanctions, but it will be more difficult for the former.

The likely impact of economic sanctions cannot be judged separately from the question of what they are intended to achieve. We must distinguish between sanctions designed to change the character of the target state and those aimed at influencing that state to abandon a particular activity. They may be a very poor method of forcing a country to change its essential nature or abandon basic national goals; but they may be quite effective when less is at stake. Sponsorship of terrorism is unlikely to be such a vital national interest that it is worth incurring the considerable popular discontent that a deteriorating economy might prompt.

Let us assume that economic and political measures (sanctions, calling in debts, diplomatic isolation) can be shown to have failed or have little chance of succeeding. Military action will need to be considered according to the criteria discussed earlier of transnationalism, openness and discrimination. This sort of strategy is best undertaken overtly because it requires the clear communication of political demands. However, in some cases the actual communications between governments may have to be private in order that the offender is not put in the position of being seen to succumb to outside pressure.

Indiscriminate reprisals following terrorist acts risk confirming a low standard of international behaviour and expanding the enemy's popular base, while alienating friends. Transnationalism refers to joint action or to dependence on others for facilities or airspace in mounting attacks. Drawing in others may be preferable in terms of public opinion, but the need for cooperation with another may lead to further compromises in designing the operation.

The operation itself must be linked to political objectives. Are targets chosen on account of their relevance to terrorist activity (training facilities, etc.), or their ability to impose extra costs on the terrorist or his sponsor, or their capacity to inflict a devastating blow that does not necessarily involve targets tied to terrorist activity but will force the offending government to rethink its policies? It may not be possible to mount the sort of attack that seems most appropriate, perhaps because of concerns over discrimination and transnationalism, or else because the targets cannot be clearly identified or are inaccessible.

There is also a high premium on success, in that failure merely improves the adversary's position (for example, the abortive American attempt to rescue the diplomatic hostages in Iran in 1980). Fear of failure, perhaps because of a malfunction in one of the systems employed (a helicopter or a missile) might encourage the counterterrorist to use more retaliatory measures than is necessary, with the result that the operation becomes cruder and blunter.

Finally, it is frequently argued that any action taken should be a *proportionate* response, implying some calculable ratio of appropriateness. Yet a true strategy of indirect influence may require a response which seems to go beyond this ratio, in that the costs to the offending country must exceed the benefits of continuing with the offence. In popular parlance the fine distinction between proportionality and equivalence may be lost. The desire to justify a response as proportionate may lead to an exaggeration of the threat posed by the state in question in order to vindicate the severity of the response—the main consequence of which will be to bolster the image of the offending state as something to be really feared.

After the US raid on Libya there was a surprising readiness to credit Colonel Gaddafi with a capacity for instant retaliation at places and by means of his own choosing, as if his tentacles could reach far and wide, and as if he had an organization ready to spring into action with an efficiency and alertness far exceeding Western special forces. In practice, even if retaliation has been ordered, unless instant and easy victims are available (as there were in the case of the UK hostages in the Lebanon), such retaliation would take weeks, if not months, to organize and would still probably be directed at 'soft' targets. The suggestion that the most likely targets would be such high-security areas as US air bases in Britain indicates again how suddenly Gaddafi's power became exaggerated by both the opponents and the proponents of this particular set of raids.

This is not to say that retaliation will *not* follow; only that the terrorist is likely to find it more difficult, and to take more time, to raise the level of his action than the counterterrorist, simply because he is probably already operating to the limits of his capability. The exception is the case of state-sponsored terrorism where the sponsoring state itself has an even more powerful backer. In practice, at least in the Middle East, the connections between governments and the different political groups, and between governments and major external powers such as the Soviet Union, are complex. The visible backing of a major power is an important asset to a government engaging in state terrorism, even if that power disapproves of the terrorism itself. The US raid on Libya became less risky when the Soviet Union visibly withdrew its support for Gaddafi; by the same token, Syria, whose responsibility for serious terrorist activity may actually be greater, was less vulnerable to a US response.

If it is the case that counterterrorist action must be disproportionate in order to persuade the target country that persisting in terrorism will be a costly business, this does not necessarily apply to the scale of the violence but could refer to the capacity to mount operations regularly over an extended period. Strategies of indirect influence depend as much on the *potential* demonstrated by actual attacks as on the attacks themselves. The expectation must be of a campaign rather than a single decisive engagement. This, however, does raise a problem for the counterterrorist version of such strategies. The terrorist is unlikely to be physically defeated, though he may be hurt. He can decide whether to continue his campaign or to retire from the fray until the fuss has died down. If he decides on the former, the counterterrorist is virtually obliged to continue his reprisals, given the message contained in his initial response. But the terrorist response may be ambiguous, or come after a long delay, or perhaps involve countries against which a robust response might be less appropriate.

Thus the greatest problem with the strategy comes when it is necessary to return to the fray. The difficulty will lie, not so much in a lack of military means, as in sustaining political support for a campaign which has already visibly failed to stop terrorism, or which—in terms of the level or character of reprisal—goes beyond what is politically tolerable. However, even a military response poses problems: having sought the most eloquent type of action to make the initial impression, will there be anything equally appropriate the second time? The first pressure having failed, is it now necessary to step it up a notch? There is unlikely to be the same possibility for surprise; in all respects the adversary may be better prepared.

The very specific set of conditions that must be met if military measures are to be even attempted indicates the difficulty of using such measures in an exemplary manner: that is, to persuade others not to put themselves at risk by offending in the same way. While that actual willingness to use force may convey a certain sort of resolve, the limitations placed on that use may allow other potential offenders to persuade themselves that they would not be punished in similar circumstances. The point is that whether or not the offender 'deserves' punishment is going to be only one of the factors determining whether it will be meted out in practice, and the offender will know that.

This does not mean that counterterrorist strategies of a military nature invariably fail. It is unwise to be dogmatic or to indulge in clichés about 'spirals of violence' on one side, or 'force is the only language they understand' on the other. The difficulty with any strategy of indirect influence is that there can be no guarantee that the victim will move in the way desired. He may be a craven coward or recklessly heroic. There can be no knowing until he is put to the test. All one can say is that a military strategy is going to be an option only in a minority of cases. It is fair also to note that although a vigorous military response may satisfy a desire for retribution, it cannot prevent further terrorism and may even make the long-term task of defeating terrorism that much harder. Groups that thrive on notoriety can only benefit from being seen to get a great power rattled.

In the end it is important to put the problem in its political context. If one is dealing with the more violent face of a broad political movement, then it will only be through a political process that one may be able to persuade the violent to follow a more peaceful path or, alternatively, persuade their erstwhile sympathizers to reject them. The more the terrorists are operating on the political fringes without effective backing the more desperate their acts will become and the more they themselves will be vulnerable to good intelligence and security measures. If there is no political process available, then one is effectively talking about a war, and survival may come to depend on an intense commitment to reduce all vulnerabilities, on the Israeli and Northern Ireland models.

However, many groups are on the political fringes and are susceptible to all the weaknesses of extremist groups: squabbles among themselves, personality cults, offensive behaviour to potential friends. In such instances it is better to play on these weaknesses than to assign the groups a political credibility that they do not deserve. Terrorism often represents an attempt at a quick military fix of a vexing political problem; when this is the case, it normally fails. When counterterrorism resorts to similar methods, it will probably face a similar fate.

6

The political dilemmas for Western governments

CHRISTOPHER HILL

It is only since the beginning of the 1980s that terrorism has begun to create major problems for West–West relations. That Western governments now recognize the need for a concerted policy on terrorism reflects changes both in Western attitudes and in terrorist practices, and to some extent is a mark of the ability of international terrorists to force a change in states' priorities.

There are two main sets of such problems: the *primary* dilemmas that face Western states (defined as developed, capitalist, liberal democracies, i.e. the OECD states) when trying to cope at a practical level with terrorism (these difficulties will be definitional, technical or institutional in the first instance, but cannot ultimately avoid political judgments); and the *secondary* dilemmas that terrorism provokes in wider areas of policy. The latter category includes attitudes to the use of force and its legitimacy; attitudes to alternative instruments such as economic sanctions; and the implications for East–West relations, Middle Eastern politics and domestic politics within the democracies.

These central issues can only be understood, however, in the light of the historical background. This is the subject of the following preamble, which ends with a close look at the common assumption that terrorism is now one of the West's principal foreign policy preoccupations.

Historical background

For most of the past decade and a half, terrorism, whether local or international (and the distinction is difficult to make), has been only a latent problem in West-West relations. There have been four reasons for this. First is the fact that the United States was not in the front line of domestic terrorist attacks during the 1970s. The Symbionese Liberation Army represented the heights of home-grown American terrorism, and it was easily contained.[1] The Black Power movement, somewhat surprisingly, given inner-city tension and the prison conditions so powerfully exposed by George Jackson in *Soledad Brother*,[2] shrivelled away under the impact of the more progressive policies on assimilation initiated by Lyndon Johnson and followed up by his successors. This lack of a domestic contact group robbed the transnationally violent of any real means of pressurizing the United States at its most sensitive points. The United States did, however, suffer not infrequently from its citizens being the targets of transnational terrorist activities, as Paul Wilkinson demonstrates. American governments were active in efforts to tighten up the international community's response, for example through the 1979 UN Convention discussed by Adam Roberts. But their concern fell far short of the more recent US moves to declare war on international terrorism as a threat to American national security.

Not that revolutionary circles wished to spare the United States, even in the Third World, where the identification of the USA with anti-colonialism had long since faded away. Indeed the Vietnam war and other radical 'causes' of the 1960s had centred attention on Washington as the major opponent of radical change in new states. Yet the very experiences of the USA in Vietnam, where it was defeated by a guerrilla insurgency, and in Latin America, where its interests were unsuccessfully challenged by guerrilla tactics, delayed the onset of anti-US terrorism. In the 1960s and 1970s, the debate on the left about how to combat American 'imperialism' was largely defined in terms of military combat, albeit of an unconventional kind. The idea of precipitating a crisis in capitalism through violent incidents such as bombings characterized intellectual anarchist groups that were active in Europe rather than in the United States.[3]

There was also the factor of time-lag. The antagonisms aroused by the various applications of the USA's containment policy and sphere-of-influence doctrines in the 1950s and 1960s took time to work through. Those alienated by the global exercise of American power after 1945 needed time to organize and to find their opportunities. Moreover, whereas time tended to dim the memories of French and British interventions, as those two states scaled down their activities outside Europe, American difficulties increased in proportion. Now clearly the greatest world power, and the most assertive apologist of capitalism, the United States was increasingly likely to suffer merely by virtue of its prominent position. The problems of salience were compounded by Washington's willingness to give unqualified support to Israel, however embattled that country became. This point will be developed further at a later stage. For the present it is enough to note that the process of Arab embitterment at the United States was largely quiescent in the 1970s, and did not come to a head until the Reagan years. Furthermore, though American citizens *were* targets of terrorism (as in some of the actions of the Red Army Faction), the incidents were seen as a series of worrying but specific events rather than as a general threat to US leadership in the international system. The pattern did not emerge, as is common enough, until the individual elements had been objectively present for some time. When it did, the reaction, inevitably, was the more fierce for the delay.

The lack of a major impact by terrorism on the United States, therefore, meant the lack of a major American response and of a potentially serious source of Western divisions. The second reason why terrorism has been largely a latent issue in Western relations until recently is the obverse of this. The Europeans were the principal sufferers, both as direct targets for attack and as the playground for demonstrations of international terrorism's capacity for action (for example, the kidnapping of OPEC ministers at Vienna in 1975). It was difficult to form a consensus even within Europe on how to deal with these activities, but at least the crucial Alliance dimension was not brought into play, thus limiting the political visibility of Western differences. Moreover, European divisions were kept in check by the fact that (give or take a few extradition disputes between Spain and France, or the Federal Republic and France) the problem was fragmented, and was internal to the individual states. The IRA was primarily a British concern, Baader-Meinhof mainly German, and the Red Brigades Italian. Connections were clearly present with Palestinian groups, as in 1976 during the hijacking of an Air France plane to Entebbe, but this posed technical more than political problems.

Only when the question of state backing for transnational terrorist activities arose, in parallel with the apparent decline of indigenous European terrorism and the expansion of Middle Eastern activities into Europe to fill the vacuum, did the possibility of serious divisions open up, both within Europe and within the Alliance. This did not happen, at least in public, until the 1980s. The evident disintegration of the Lebanon seemed explanation enough at first for the ease with which military groups could form, and establish bases. It is true that the use of Europe as a theatre of terrorist operations inevitably involved American personnel who were working in US firms abroad and NATO bases (and of course was intended to do so). But damage of this kind was essentially collateral from a Washington perspective. America seemed to be caught up in European problems, more than being the recipients of a direct challenge. Attacks on Israel, the close ally, were abhorred but seen as part of the struggle which that country had to conduct on many fronts to survive in the Middle East. Japan and other non-European allies, moreover, were largely immune from terrorist attacks (although Japan produced some of the most fanatical international terrorists).

The third factor which kept terrorism from becoming a major problem was the very success of Western governments in prophylaxis—or, rather, 'containment', for terrorism survived in one form or another whatever its opponents did. But there is no doubt that the activities of dedicated terrorists were considerably restricted by countermanoeuvres as the 1970s came to an end. The Baader-Meinhof group was suppressed, the Red Brigades thrown very much on the defensive, and even the IRA forced into more conventional politics in an attempt to avoid the isolation sought by Westminster. Aircraft hijackings, moreover, seemed to be on the decrease as the lessons of terrorist success at Dawson's Field in 1970, and failure at Entebbe in 1976, were absorbed. European special forces, indeed, were going 'out of area' to end hijackings, as with the German operation at Mogadishu in 1977, when a Lufthansa jet was stormed and 86 hostages freed. Far from inducing complacency on the part of Western officials, this success seems to have led to a steady improvement in security measures at Western embassies throughout the period. As a result, terrorism was kept in a compartment, intellectual and political, several levels down from the key issues discussed at seven-nation summits or in bilateral exchanges between the United States and its allies.

The fourth and last reason relates to deliberate policy decisions. In general the Western response to terrorism in the first, major phase of 1968–79 was to oppose it firmly but also to play down the *strategic* threat. The approach was designed to break down the problem into its separate components and thereby make it more manageable. To raise the temperature to the level of crisis would have been, it seemed, to play into the hands of the terrorists, whose very intention was to put target societies into a state of siege, to polarize public opinion within them and to focus attention on themselves. Whereas in 1947 Marshall and Truman had felt that the American public would accept a global foreign policy only by being 'scared' into it, Western governments in the 1970s wanted at all costs to make terrorists seem marginal and bizarre, not a major challenge to existing values, while at the same time hoping for maximum public vigilance and assistance in police operations against them.

The Israelis, it is true, took a different line, but they were the exception that proved the rule, partly because Israel is effectively at war with the Palestinians, and partly because other Western states were happy enough to let Israel try the mailed-fist option first, and relieved to have them draw terrorist fire. More subtly, the Europeans in particular came increasingly to define their own attitudes on these matters in contradistinction to those of the Israelis. Even the United States, although undoubtedly a source of considerable assistance to Israel in this as in most other spheres, was probably not dissatisfied at being able for once to keep below the parapet, in the service trenches.

In short, until recently, terrorism has not contrived to drive serious wedges between individual states or between the United States and the Europeans as a whole. To what extent has this situation changed fundamentally?

Recent developments

Ever since President Carter's Camp David initiative (1978), the United States has increasingly been the target of radical Arab opponents of Israel. Encouraged by the 'rejectionist front' of states who dissociated themselves from Anwar Sadat's deal with

Menachem Begin at Camp David, those in the Palestinian movement who distrusted Yassir Arafat's diplomatic strategy came to
believe in direct action against Israel's most resolute backer. The
turn of events against the United States, which was to have such
important and wide-ranging effects, therefore began well before
Ronald Reagan's election as president, and his tougher talk (and
eventual action) against those who used terror as a weapon.

The Iranian revolution accelerated these developments and
created significant links between Islamic fundamentalists based in
Lebanon and Khomeini's regime (ironically despite Israel's own
links with Iran after the onset of the Gulf war in 1980). What
followed is the now familiar chronicle of outrages against targets
which more and more tended to have an American component or
denomination. And the very fact that the United States had now
become the main target for Middle Eastern terrorist attacks (the
more so because of Israel's own relentlessly effective security
measures, particularly those of the *El Al* airline) thrust terrorism to
the forefront of policy debate in all the Western states. However the
USA reacted to attacks on its citizens, indifference was the one
response which could be safely ruled out. And once Washington had
evinced concern on an issue, its allies automatically took notice.

They could hardly avoid doing so during the prolonged agony of
the American hostages seized in Tehran, which dominated the last
year of President Carter's term of office. This episode is relevant here
only in so far as it illustrates the important truth that a terrorist
attack on an American target (especially in or close to Europe)
presents a problem for the Europeans over and above their genuine
concern to see hostages freed or lives saved: namely, they have to
cope with the USA's response, which is bound to have wide
repercussions, whatever form it takes. In this case, the Europeans,
while undoubtedly indispensable to Washington in many behind-
the-scenes ways, clearly spent much of their time in a damage-
limitation exercise, trying first to prevent economic sanctions being
forced upon them, then heading off US military action and finally
damping down the sanctions which were agreed. In between times,
the anger felt in the US at this caution was matched by the
Europeans' resentment that their own eventual agreement to sanctions had been used as a cover by the US for the rescue mission,
which began the day after the European measures were announced
(shades of the 1986 raid on Libya).

Since the end of the hostage crisis (and the associated demise of Carter), the changes in terrorist actions and aims which the crisis prefigured have led to an increasing concentration on American targets, particularly in 1985–6. The United States itself, however, has proved too far from the Middle East, and too difficult to enter, for terrorists to be able to threaten Americans in their home cities; it is Americans in Europe and the Mediterranean who have been at risk. The change has been matched, and indeed has itself partly led to, an ever more robust American attitude towards military counter-measures. This is related to the new willingness to use troops abroad in limited warfare, as in the Lebanon (1982–4) or Grenada (1983), but the determination to 'fight' terrorism has led in particular to the search for identifiable targets. This search ended (whether temporarily we cannot know) with the attacks on Libya in April 1986.

The Libyan attacks were merely the most dramatic manifestation of the difference between the United States and its European friends which the terrorism issue had been eliciting throughout the 1980s. Despite the fact that Reagan was being criticized by his own right wing for talking loudly but doing little, the Europeans were already considerably alarmed by his stance. A polarization of views on many subjects, but particularly on East-West relations and the Middle East, was becoming semi-permanent in a way that was new to the NATO Alliance. The growing assertiveness of Europeans on foreign policy issues, expressed through the framework of European Political Cooperation (EPC, dealing largely with the harmonization of national foreign policies), was not welcome in Washington when it amounted to a strategy for constraining the US, as it has increasingly done. The enlargement of the EC to include Greece, and later Spain and Portugal, has hardly strengthened the voices of those inclined to support American counter-attacks on terrorism. In short, the re-emergence of terrorism as a major foreign policy dilemma has quickly spilled over into other areas of disagreement and has complicated, if not exacerbated, them.

To end this historical preamble, we should pose a cautionary question: are these difficulties likely to be a *permanent* feature of West-West relations? On the one hand, it is by no means certain that the revival of dramatic terrorist attacks represents a reversal of the underlying trend towards the containment, or stabilization at an 'acceptable' level, of terrorism. The various groups involved in such activities are still divided among themselves, Western security forces are among the most efficient in the world (even leaving aside the constraints of operating in pluralist societies) and political conditions may yet change in ways which will reduce the incentive for terrorism, if not remove it altogether. If this is so, then one important source of Western division will be diminished. On the other hand, if incidents such as those at Rome and Vienna airports in December 1985 continue at regular intervals, the potential for clashes between security forces—epitomized by the stand-off between the US Delta Force and Italian armed police in Sicily after the hijack of the liner *Achille Lauro* in the autumn of 1985—will be increased. Given the dramatic media coverage which is inevitable in such events (which, indeed, is one of the main reaons why the act of terrorism is committed), public responses are inevitable, and discrepant ones at that—not only because of the considerable variations between American and European attitudes, but also because of differences within Europe (witness French responses to the raid on Libya). If *this* chain of events takes place, then the wave of terrorist attacks which began in 1985 will have undermined Western unity in a way which did not prove possible in the 1970s—but only because now, in the mid-1980s, the fissures are already there to exploit.

The primary dilemmas

Of the many dilemmas that now face Western governments in their primary task of coping with terrorist activities, the first is the sheer difficulty of defining the problem. Terrorists may be seen variously as criminals, lunatics, fanatics, nihilists or simply political actors of a particular type, although, as often as not, they combine elements of all of these. Competing definitions of terrorism, and of the problem it poses, are clearly an important factor in dividing the United States from some of its allies, with the former tending to see the terrorist more as an incomprehensible, atavistic, threat to civilization, and the Europeans emphasizing the historical origins of terrorist behaviour.

This dichotomy is, of course, grossly oversimplified. Serious people in the administrations of all major countries, not least the

United States, are only too well aware of the complexities of terrorism and the contexts in which it occurs. But, at the level of public debate, simplification is inevitable, and on this issue, at this time, the dominant simplifications do divide on transatlantic lines, with consequential strains.

Even at the declaratory level, however, there is a broad level of agreement on essentials: namely, that we cannot risk legitimizing terrorism (difficult cases like the African National Congress are generally avoided), and that the phenomenon has therefore to be defined as a form of pathology. On the other hand, two different types of double-think are at work. The US tends to regard terrorists as, at the same time, inhuman fanatics and (implicitly) rational actors who will respond to acts of deterrence. The Europeans, for their part, tend to eschew the use of force (except against terrorists caught *in flagrante*) on the grounds that it will only set up a cycle of reaction and counterreaction. They prefer to concentrate on eroding the 'root causes' of terrorism, yet do not have any instruments other than diplomacy available to help restructure the conditions out of which violence has sprung. Preventive measures can go only so far. These contradictions are unfortunately not symmetrical, and inevitably lead to considerable misunderstandings at the most basic of levels. Neither view would expect terrorism to be extirpatable, but whereas the one definition tends to narrow down the options for response to various forms of coercion, the other leads to an emphasis on long-term strategies to which acts of reprisal, and even deterrence, are *always* likely to be impediments.

The question of identifying the sources of terrorism, particularly the state sources, is perhaps the most obvious of the dilemmas which have beset Western governments. There are two aspects to this: (i) Are states at all significantly responsible for terror, or is it principally the product of independent, transnational, groups? (ii) To the extent that states are responsible, which are the principal culprits?

On the first of these issues, there have been differences within national administrations. It is inherently unclear whether the fact that militant Palestinians depend on states for camp facilities, visas and financial support, means that their hosts can control any terrorist activities which might be pursued. It is even more uncertain whether the professional underground terrorist units, with no obvious base, can be used or constrained by states sympathetic to them. The most that can be said is that the ambiguity of the facts creates wide margins for wishful thinking, and therefore disagreement, among the states on the receiving end of terrorism. All governments, by definition, find it difficult to grasp the nature and extent of the transnational dimension of terrorism, and tend to assume that other governments must be implicated in hostile activities—particularly when evidence is turned up of weapons being carried in diplomatic bags. On the other hand, it is not convenient to have too much clear evidence implicating third states, since that makes some kind of action difficult to evade.

In the event, the question of general state responsibility for terrorism can hardly be divorced from the arguments over the involvement of particular states. Despite the increasing tendency of experts to conclude that terrorists are largely autonomous actors, the unprovability of such a proposition provides many opportunities for branding certain opponents as guilty parties. Thus the United States found it convenient to focus attention on Libya as a means of dealing with a problem which (as in the Lebanon) it had found intractable, despite the fact that Colonel Gaddafi was only one of a number of possible sources of support for terrorism. Conversely, accusations of the Soviet Union's deep involvement in terrorist activities have significantly died away in American official circles as the possibilities of a major arms control agreement with Moscow have increased, and as the USSR has shown itself more willing to condemn terrorism. In such matters the evidence, or lack of it, about a state's involvement is very much secondary to the wider context of international and domestic politics. This certainly explains why Syria has not been put under the searchlight by Washington despite its present bullish attitudes.

So much for the definitional aspects. The next category, technical coordination, is the most down-to-earth of the problems facing governments trying to devise strategies for dealing with terrorism, although it is none the easier to solve for that. Coordination is a standard problem in foreign policy-making, both internally and internationally. In the nature of things, it is extremely difficult to glean information about degrees of efficiency in such a sensitive area of state operations as counterterrorism. It is clear that inter-agency rivalries have been intense, notwithstanding the security status of the problem, the downwards pressure for consistency which must be coming from the highest levels of government, and the centralized administrative traditions of societies like Britain and France. Operational personnel tend to be impatient of bureaucratic procedures, and diplomats to be alarmed at the tendency of security experts to treat rules as disposable. The *Rainbow Warrior* affair, in late summer 1985, when French agents sank a Greenpeace vessel in a New Zealand harbour, illustrated this tension perfectly and reduced French decision-making, for a time, to a shambles.

Evidence of this kind certainly supports the wealth of academic documentation about the prevalence of bureaucratic politics even in 'high policy' matters. On the other hand, if we judge by results, then it is clear that maladministration is by no means universal. The United States, despite its well-known tendency to bureaucratic fragmentation, has a good record in protecting its own society, airports and foreign bases against attack, even if it is incapable of ensuring the safety of all Americans abroad all of the time. (Indeed fragmentation may improve security in some respects, if it restricts the flow of information.) Britain and West Germany fall into the same category, although tough emergency powers may have been as important as effective coordination in enhancing security, with the concomitant costs in terms of civil liberties. Other states, however, such as Belgium, France and Greece, have probably been somewhat less successful so far in tightening up their administrative systems so that information is shared, blocking tactics avoided and objectives clarified. Institutional jealousies proliferate. These can lead to intra-European irritations that are quite as important as the transatlantic tensions that exist on other aspects of the terrorist question.

So far as coordination between states is concerned, the problem can be addressed in terms of a familiar general dilemma in international relations, namely what group to associate with and for what purpose. This is not simply a matter of optimum group-size, or of finding partners who are reliable (although neither criterion can be discounted). It is about working positively with those who share one's own definition of the problem, while not conceding effective vetoes to those who do not by bringing them inside the collective policy process. At the same time, those who share certain vital interests, but start from a different perspective, have to be persuaded to cooperate where possible and not to take too much disruptive action of their own.

The practical consequences of these general, but important, considerations have been that the most populous and wide-ranging organization of potential relevance to the terrorist problem, Interpol, is not the main framework for cooperation as far as the major Western states are concerned, despite its aspirations to this status. This is partly because European police forces do not want to share information with Eastern bloc countries, or indeed Libya, which are all members, and partly because Interpol was, at least until 1984, constitutionally limited to action on criminal matters (states disagree about whether terrorism can be kept in a separate category from ordinary crime).[4] Moreover, Interpol is riven by disputes, short of resources and too big. Fortunately, other large international organizations can produce action within a limited scope. The International Maritime Organization and the International Civil Aviation Organization have both made some progress towards common procedures at sea and in the air respectively. But coordination of this kind can be no more than a slow, fitful business in a universal organization.

At the other end of the spectrum, the seven-nation economic summits have become increasingly concerned with political issues over the years, and in consequence have recently turned to the problem of terrorism. The declaration which came out of the Tokyo summit in May 1986 was hailed at the time as a major charter for action, but it has subsequently become clear that some signatories regard it as merely a general demonstration of solidarity, which commits them to few practical changes of policy. Such agreements doubtless have some practical value in that they breed an awareness of the importance of maintaining an overall consensus on an issue, but they are so imbued with the spirit of linkage politics and package-deals as to be essentially inappropriate for achieving major progress on a single, complicated problem like terrorism.

It is at the intermediate level that there has probably been most success, in the sense that mechanisms have been created which satisfy the professional and appear to produce tolerable results. The Council of Europe has been important in the juridical field. It produced the European Convention on the Suppression of Terrorism (1977), the existence of which has fostered a climate in which further cooperation has been made possible, albeit in the more intimate and flexible environment of the European Community.[5] Bilateral relations, of course, are likely to be even closer and more effective, whether between pairs of European states, or between the United States and its major allies (some being more trusted than others). In such a framework, informal cooperation must go some way towards obviating the normal problems of communication between the state apparatuses, with all their cumbersome formalities. Such cooperation is especially likely over dramatic single events such as the assassination of Swedish Prime Minister Olaf Palme in February 1986. By contrast, wide-membership organizations like the Council of Europe can easily seem too unwieldy and lacking in security to be worth using.

The opposite danger, however, must not be forgotten: namely, that the intimacy of a 'special relationship' can actually damage the overall pattern of international cooperation by simply reconstructing the parochialisms of a nationalistic approach at the joint level. The assumption, in this case, is that only the privileged partner can be trusted, and that further dilution cannot be risked.

It was probably with dangers of this kind in mind that in 1976, after heavy IRA attacks in London and the seizure of the German embassy in Stockholm, the members of the European Community set up, on a British initiative, what has become known as the 'Trevi' system of working-groups.[6] This operates alongside EPC and has a similar structure, but is not part of the foreign policy consultations themselves. It has its own telex network, does not involve the Commission, and is not affected by the recent incorporation of EPC into the legal structure of the Community via the Single European Act (1986). Most important, Trevi is not headed by Ministers of Foreign Affairs. It consists of representatives of Ministries of the Interior, police forces, and security services, and is answerable to those ministers in member-states who are responsible for counterterrorism (this may be Ministers of the Interior or Ministers of Justice, depending on the state). These ministers now meet once during every six-month Presidency, and the expert working-groups prepare their agendas. The precise composition and activities of the groups are secret, but secrecy alone cannot account for the fact that diplomats on the EPC circuit (which itself regularly deals with the foreign policy ramifications of terrorism) do not always know who their national representative on Trevi is. Once again, bureaucratic parochialism plays its part.

The lack of effective coordination has clearly been felt in the most important area of all, that of relations between the technical and the political approaches to the question of terrorism. In January 1986, in response to heightened tension over Libya (and thereby in Euro-

89

American relations), a new working-group was set up in EPC to deal with the political complexities. By inference, Trevi has been able to meet the requirements of those concerned with operational matters well enough (although new arrangements have had to be made to stimulate meetings between the police chiefs of the European airports in the front line). It has not, however, managed to deal adequately with the more fundamental questions of defining objectives, maintaining consensus—and handling the United States.

Trevi is considered a success by its political masters as well as its practitioners—so much so that non-EC members have wanted to become associated with it. Special arrangements have been made for the US and interested West European states (but not Japan). It is largely a self-sustaining process, which brings evident dangers of complacency and introspection, with ministerial anxiety producing only an occasional spur. Yet even for Trevi, perhaps the most successful mechanism for cooperation against international terrorism yet produced by states (if we are to accept the European view at its own value), there are two fundamental problems which are unlikely to be fully overcome.

One is the continuing divergence of national interests and perceptions, here as in every aspect of the Community's life. Despite the crises over Libya in 1984 and 1986, for example, Britain has not been able to persuade its partners that Libya is a sufficiently serious threat to European order to justify the shutting down of all Libyan missions and the expulsion of all Libyan personnel. Not all states (including Britain, perhaps) even accept that Libya is to blame as often as is alleged. Italy, France and Greece certainly have vested interests—intensified by their geographical situation—in thinking not. Even the Federal Republic of Germany has important commercial interests at stake.[7]

The second obstacle is that a proper common policy on counter-terrorism would require a judicial integration of a kind that is decades away. The different systems and philosophies of law, quite apart from extradition laws and attitudes to political refugees, have so far stopped the rhetoric about a 'common European judicial space' from being translated into any very serious practical action, despite the ebb and flow of working-groups on the subject. Indeed, so far as these issues are being pursued, they are being quite properly dealt with in the 21-member Council of Europe. A common EC policy would profit little if guilty parties were simply able to seek sanctuary in Sweden (say) rather than France. Such considerations, however, will probably not prevent further demarcation disputes between the two European institutions.

Ultimately, no single organization can be used for intergovernmental cooperation on terrorism. It is a question, as usual in international relations, of keeping all the balls in the air while concentrating on the patterns woven by an inner few. Trevi and the EC can provide a model, perhaps a lead, for Western states concerned to harmonize policies, but they can hardly follow a *sauve qui peut* line even on this collective basis. Certainly the balance struck between groups, and within them, will continue to provide states with serious dilemmas, partly practical but also of a deeply political nature, both in the prevention and in the treatment of terrorist attacks.

Secondary dilemmas

The intermingling of the practical and the political leads us from the direct business of handling terrorism into its wider ramifications. As a problem of foreign policy, terrorism both complicates other areas of comparable importance, and is complicated by them. We shall look briefly at three of the most relevant of these areas: the role of force in the prosecution of Western foreign policies; the conduct of policy on what the superpowers have agreed to designate 'regional' problems, i.e. disputes away from the main European theatre, particularly in the Middle East; and the domestic context of foreign policy, particularly in the United States and Western Europe.

The use of military force is steadily becoming a major source of division in the Western Alliance, and terrorism has helped to sharpen the sense of it. All parties, of course, agree in principle that force is a last resort, but that it may have to be used in certain, highly regrettable, circumstances. In the past ten years the French and the British have both taken up arms with no greater compunction than the United States. The rub comes, however, in circumstances more common than the French problems in Zaire in 1977 and 1978, or Britain's war for the Falklands in 1982. Should troops be used for reasons of punishment, deterrence or local balance of power (so long as there is little risk of direct conflict with the Soviet Union), in areas of the Third World in which vital Western interests can be argued to be at stake? This question has run through the postwar period of the American 'rise to globalism', and the varying answers have usually had major consequences—whether at Suez in 1956, the Lebanon in 1958, Cuba in 1961 and 1962, Angola in 1976 and Libya in 1986, to give just a few examples.

At present, thirty years on from Suez, there is no clear schism discernible on this issue, even between the Europeans and Reaganite America. France took the strongest action of all the Western peacekeeping forces in the Lebanon during 1983–4, and French opinion was not hostile to the US strike against Libya in 1986, despite Mitterrand's ban on the F-111s' overflight. On the other hand, it is possible to detect in Europe a certain ennui, a distaste for the prospect of military operations, overt and covert, which is not currently seen in the United States. Whether because of an historical fatigue with war or sheer lack of capability, European governments now display a diplomatic reflex when faced with problems which might once have called forth a military response. Except in the event of an attack on actual French or British possessions, which is now becoming ever less likely as Britain rapidly divests itself of its few remaining colonies, it is difficult to conceive of European forces now being committed out of area except in a peacekeeping capacity.

This also applies to a large extent to the United States, although the use in 1983–4 of the battleship *New Jersey* off the Lebanon, and the Libyan raid, suggest that it is difficult for a superpower to renounce its obvious comparative advantage. Revisionism with regard to the Vietnam war has not yet gone so far as to commit American troops even to the fighting close to home in Nicaragua and El Salvador. Moreover, in a longer perspective, it may seem that the United States was surprisingly slow to respond militarily to terrorist attacks on its citizens, given the known views of Reagan and his supporters. Nonetheless, if the reactions to terrorism have in the last analysis made clearer the differences in attitude to the use of force as an instrument of foreign policy which undoubtedly exist within the Alliance, then terrorism has also led to closer definitions of the circumstances in which force might be productive, perhaps thereby laying down the basis for a new Western consensus. The reference here is to the tendency, clear in modern American strategy, to avoid the formal commitment of troops, and certainly to avoid the mass deployment which in Vietnam provided guerrilla opponents with their most desired target. Instead, 'covert' (i.e. unofficial and dispersed) or highly limited operations are undertaken, preferably in countries in which US efforts are on the side of the destabilizing, rather than the stabilizing, forces.

For their part, the Europeans are not too unhappy with this development. Proxy conflicts are less dangerous than direct confrontations while the United States takes the lead and bears the brunt of the criticism. It may even be that quiet assistance can be given by European special forces at little cost and with considerable political gain in terms of goodwill earned in Washington. The problems arise only when American and European interpretations of the terms 'terrorists' and 'freedom-fighters' do not coincide (as in the case of Nicaragua), and—more important for our purposes—when US operations against international terrorists (as over Libya in 1986) seem more likely to sow dragon's teeth than to help resolve the problem. If, however, US strikes of this kind are infrequent and well-judged (in the sense that their efforts are related to their objectives), it may be that European criticisms will be disarmed, muted by the perception of a free ride.

Attitudes to the alternatives to military force are the mirror-image of what we have already observed, at least so far as diplomacy is concerned. In general the European states prefer to pursue a diplomatic solution, first, second and last, while the United States has become increasingly uneasy about the thin line between negotiation and 'appeasement', contrasting the low productivity of diplomacy (Camp David was, after all, the despised President Carter's achievement) with what has flowed from Israel's direct action.

Economic sanctions, however, lead to more ambivalent reactions, for they combine diplomacy and coercion in the same strategy. Opposition to sanctions has virtually become a principle for Margaret Thatcher and Ronald Reagan. Yet both leaders wish to exert pressure on Libya because of its presumed involvement in terrorism. The Danes and the Benelux countries would probably go along with sanctions, but only if it were a way of heading off further American military action. The southern Europeans, on the other hand, have too much at stake in their economic and cultural ties with the Maghreb to want to risk breaking off trade with Libya. The terrorism issue, therefore, has done little to unify an already divided West on the utility of economic sanctions; indeed, it has probably complicated the question further. The only consolation in this respect is that Libya is the sole case likely to attract calls for sanctions. Syria and Iran are both too important strategically to the United States for Washington to take the initiative, and the Europeans have already made it clear that they do not accept the USA's tendency to equate terrorism with the policies of all radical leftist regimes in Latin America and the Caribbean. For the present, this particular aspect of the dispute over sanctions remains quiescent.

Regional issues

The next set of secondary dilemmas involves those big issues of international politics that are incidentally, if inevitably, affected by acts of terror. These fall largely into the category of 'regional' issues, for West-West relations have remained unshaken by the dramatic events under discussion—if precariously on such occasions as the attempted assassination of John Paul II. There is a circular process at work here, for most of the truly international terrorist activities, particularly in recent years, have grown out of 'regional' theatres, especially the Middle East. The place of the Middle East in the growth of international terrorism is dealt with in Chapter 3 by Philip Windsor. What is of interest in this context is the extent to which terrorism has become detached from the central issues of the Arab-Israeli conflict itself, and has thereby fed back into that conflict in a disruptive way. Instead of being, as its proponents see it, simply one form of military action in a long-running war, terrorism has become a superordinate point of issue requiring some kind of resolution of its own. In this sense the targets of terrorism have been able to determine the level of its significance. It is certainly the case that Israel, by labelling the PLO inherently terrorist, has managed to link the question of terrorism intimately to that of the regional state system. The result—which is not wholly in Israel's interests—is immobilism on both fronts.

The evidence of the past year or so suggests that both the superpowers have been resisting this linkage. The USSR appears to have tacitly approved the isolation of Libya, if not actual attacks upon it, while the United States has clearly preferred to focus its accusations of fostering terrorism on Gaddafi, being much less aggressive in its attitude towards Syria, whose influence is a crucial factor in the Levant's balance of power. Less surprisingly, the Europeans have been reluctant to allow terrorism to damage their relations with any Arab state, even Libya, when it could be avoided. They have preferred to deal with terrorist incidents as they occur, and on their own terms, resisting a model of clear state sponsorship.

The other side of the coin is the fact that the superpowers have not been able to call the shots. The Soviet Union has not (although it is difficult to tell) managed to restrain Syria's support for terrorist groups, while the United States and France—in their attempt to stabilize the Lebanon—have suffered grievously through suicide attacks. Terrorist attacks forced President Reagan to abandon his Lebanon policy, and there can be little doubt that American policy in the Middle East is now at the mercy of non-state actors. Any strategy that attempts to go beyond unquestioning support for Israel is liable to be derailed by opponents willing to use violence to sidetrack the parties. And the region is running over with groups sufficiently dedicated in their distrust of the US and Israel to ensure that this happens.

As a result, the USA and Western Europe have found that their painfully constructed attempts to create positive movement in the crucial 'shatterbelt' of the Middle East are becoming increasingly vulnerable to the tangential attacks of terrorist groups that can be controlled neither by clients nor by adversaries, but that work in the interstices of the state system. This is precisely what the terrorists intend. The final alarming irony is that the United States appears to have concluded that this type of activity works, and is supporting the Contra 'freedom-fighters' in Nicaragua along not dissimilar lines to Syrian or Iranian support for 'terrorists' in the Lebanon. Here is another indirect but nonetheless serious consequence of the emergence of terrorism as an international issue.

The domestic dimensions

We now come to the last of our secondary dilemmas: the complications created for foreign policy by the fact that terrorists make targets of ordinary citizens and therefore turn them into vitally interested parties. The domestic pressures that inevitably follow make action a major priority for the principal governments affected, whatever the delicacy of the international situation. For example, although up to mid-1985 it seemed as if the Reagan administration, despite sore temptation, was refraining from inappropriate military action, with hindsight it now seems that the USA had been biding its time and preparing to strike against Libya for demonstrative purposes. The raid, when it happened, was partly the product of the philosophy that only military force, through its deterrent effect, would be able to reduce the incidence of terrorism. But it was also the action of a populist President meeting a perceived need to satisfy an aroused public. The US government in 1985–6 has been at least as concerned to avoid the appearance of inaction as to focus on the full complexities of the terrorist question. It should be added that Washington may not have been committed to a full-scale attack on Tripoli and Benghazi until shortly before the event. The United States sent fairly clear signals to Libya through such graduated measures as its naval manoeuvres in the Gulf of Sirte. But whether these were genuine attempts at low-cost deterrence, or, rather, softening-up exercises intended to prepare the ground for the strike against Gaddafi himself, remains unclear. Moreover, graduated measures are inherently difficult to control, and can slip imperceptibly into escalation—not least when the target of the signals is deemed by the signaller to be beyond reason.

In terms of domestic politics, the needs of European governments have been almost precisely the reverse of President Reagan's: that is, there would still be pressures on them to condemn the USA's use of force, even if it could be demonstrated that it was having a deterrent effect. As we saw earlier, there does seem to be a clear division between American opinion's support for military responses, and an increasing antipathy in Europe to the use of state power in circumstances in which the innocent are at risk. This division is compounded by increasing anti-Reaganism in Europe and impatience with European 'disloyalty' in the US. Certainly domestic pressures are creating different sets of priorities among the major Western states with regard to terrorism, in a way which is unusual in foreign policy and which is producing the classic conditions for mutual misperception. When one leader does not know whether another is acting on the basis of internal or external needs, communication can easily break down. Nonetheless, terrorism and its effects are highly unpredictable, and the present pattern of differentiated domestic attitudes should not be regarded as set in stone.

Conclusions

It is obvious that terrorism as a phenomenon, rather like drug abuse or pollution, has become a major preoccupation of Western governments over the past fifteen years. Most communiqués issuing from summit meetings make reference to it and strive to give the impression of coming up with new measures that might increase security against attacks. The issue here, however, is whether or not terrorism has become a serious source of division between Western states, particularly the United States and Western Europe. The burden of the analysis has been that in itself terrorism has raised new problems, but problems that loom large only because of pre-existing difficulties in the Alliance. Even the more technical of the 'primary' dilemmas have the potential for sharp political conflict, because most of the key decisions involve political judgments about whom to cooperate with, what restriction on civil liberties to allow, and how much national autonomy to surrender in the interests of harmonized procedure. Such judgments hinge on presumptions of goodwill and definitions of partnerhsip. When we move on to the clearly political questions, to do with the origins of terrorism and its susceptibility to control, we see straightaway that it would take a particularly stable period of consensus on international policy for a large group of sovereign states to be able to agree.

The past decade has not been such a period for the Atlantic Alliance, and the old NATO 'bargain' has come under real strain. In the post-Vietnam years, the United States and its allies have gone through as many internal crises as external challenges. Moreover, although internal and external difficulties are intertwined, terrorism has not been the main source of strain. If coping with Libya, the PLFP and the IRA, among others, were the Alliance's only major problems, Western leaders would not be too concerned about the threat to solidarity. It is only because of terrorism's impact on a structure already weakened by endless arguments over nuclear weapons, arms expenditure and detente that it appears to be a dangerous solvent. Usually a common enemy unites, but terrorists are not an identifiable enemy. Their relationship with other states is elusive in the extreme, and their own identity is polycephalous. They present a moving target at which to fire is to risk self-inflicted wounds through ricochet.

Terrorism has thus exacerbated existing tensions among Western states. It may not always do so in the future, for its very hetero-geneity is likely to produce a varying pattern of challenge, with periods in which terrorist groups are less active or more divided, and Western states correspondingly more united. The transnational processes that are so difficult for states to come to terms with are not always such an advantage for the terrorists themselves. The invisibility of their leadership, and their lack of a single structure of decision-making, mean that states find political responses such as divide-and-rule impossible even to set up. But these conditions also make it difficult for one militant group to count on the support of others in any grand strategy, and the diversity of interests may lead to the frequent disappearance of cells, either as a result of repression or even because there has been an acceptable movement towards goals (e.g. the FLQ in Canada).[8]

In their turn, the divisions of the West on wider issues make collaboration against terrorism difficult to achieve, although one should probably not underestimate what is done informally, below the political level, by the freemasonry of experts—a case of limited functionalism! However, terrorists can play on the divisions that seem to paralyse collective decision-making only in a very crude manner. The time-lags and obstacles involved in setting up major terrorist attacks are not conducive to taking advantage of states' problems in other areas. The IRA did not, or could not, do much to add to Mrs Thatcher's difficulties during the Falklands war, for example.

As long as international terrorism persists, therefore, it is likely to be a serious, but not necessarily devastating, addition to the problems that beset an unwieldy group of states like NATO, let alone 'the West'. This is particularly so given that terrorism is always likely to have a strong out-of-area component, and is therefore liable to reactivate long-running debates to do with the legitimacy of intervention, the utility of force and the geographical scope of Western interests. By doing so, however, it makes clear the wider context in which terrorism must be assessed: that of our interna-tional society and its fundamental fragility.

Hysteria over terrorism only serves to disguise the dangerous problems that would continue to threaten peace if terrorism subsided tomorrow, such as the place of Israel in the Middle Eastern regional system, the increasing divide between the comfortable and satisfied and the poor and enraged, and the process of rapid change in new states. Like Chernobyl, terrorism affects and alarms us all, but it does not reach down to the water-table of the international system.

Notes

1. The Symbionese Liberation Army was responsible for the notorious kidnapping of newspaper heiress Patty Hearst in 1974. It, and other revolutionary movements such as the Weathermen and the Black Panthers, had virtually ceased operations by the late 1970s. See William Regis Farrell, *The US Government Response to Terrorism: In Search of an Effective Strategy* (Boulder, CO, Westview Press, 1982), esp. pp. 2 and 69–80. On the question of American vulnerability to international terrorism (i.e. outside the US), the statistics are even less reliable than in other areas of social science. Categories are unclear and political loading a great temptation. CIA statistics suggest that the US provided between 30% and 40% of the overall total of terrorist targets in the 1970s, but this figure is dubious because of the confusion in the measures used between, on the one hand, the total number of 'incidents' and, on the other, the 'attacks' suffered by 'US citizens or property'. See, for example, *International Terrorism in 1979* (Washington, DC, National Foreign Assessment Center, CIA, April 1980), pp. 15–16. Interestingly enough, once the terrorist question became more politicized in the 1980s, the State Department took over the yearly publication of data on terrorism, and dropped both the time-series on incidents/attacks in the 1970s *and* the dual formulation, referring thenceforward only to 'incidents'. See *Patterns of Global Terrorism: 1983* (Washington, DC, Department of State, September 1984).
2. George Jackson, *Soledad Brother: The Prison Letters of George Jackson* (London, Jonathan Cape and Penguin Books, 1971).
3. The background to the Paris events of 1968, and the rise of the Angry Brigade in Britain and the Baader-Meinhof group in West Germany, is contained in Gordon Carr, *The Angry Brigade* (London, Gollancz, 1975).
4. David Marsh, 'Interpol takes a step out of the shadows', *The Financial Times*, 15 July 1986, makes clear Interpol's concern not to be excluded from counterterrorist work by other agencies. The major states of the EC are equally determined to exclude it, seeing an

organization with 138 members as inherently unsuited to the fight against terrorism.

5. See Juliet Lodge (ed.), *Terrorism: A Challenge to the State* (Oxford, Martin Robertson, 1981). The editor's own chapter, 'The European Community and Terrorism: Establishing the Principle of "Extradite or Try"', pp. 164–94, is a useful analysis of the impact of the Convention's impact on the EC, although it concentrates on the European Parliament at the expense of Trevi.

6. Of the little published on Trevi, by far the most useful is Philippe de Schoutheete's *La Coopération Politique Européenne* (Brussels, Labor, 1980). Chapter 6 is entitled 'Le Terrorisme et l'Espace Judiciaire Européen'.

7. *Middle East Economic Digest*, 26 April 1986: 'Libya: EEC reaction underlines divisions'.

8. The FLQ, or Front de Libération du Québec, was particularly active in 1970–1, when it murdered a Canadian minister and kidnapped the British diplomat James Cross. Since then, the capacity of Prime Minister Pierre Trudeau and Québécois leader René Lévesque for judicious compromise has cut the ground from beneath the forces of violence. See John Fitzmaurice, *Québec and Canada* (London, Hurst, 1985), pp. 57–8.

7

Concluding observations

R. J. VINCENT

It has been said that it is a small victory for the champions of order that the word 'terrorism' is most often used to describe revolutionary violence.[1] Our concern in this book has been, not to do what we can to produce a bigger win for order, but to consider the range of challenges to the rules and conventions of international society stemming not only from revolutionary violence, but across the spectrum to the terrorism aimed at maintaining an established position. It is the challenge presented by the methods of terrorism, its strategy or tactics, that we have sought to isolate, even when we have gone on to say that these are intelligible only in the political context which led to the choice of them, and not other means, in the first place.

The challenge, we have seen, is not a novel one. But the revolution in mass communication has given the propaganda of the deed a global arena in which to work. And there is a sense in which the stability of boundaries in contemporary international politics has forced groups that are dissatisfied with the territorial distribution into the transnational world, where their cases might receive a more sympathetic hearing than in the society of states. When Philip Windsor suggests that the modern phenomenon of terrorism has become legitimized in the Middle East, he might mean that it has taken over from war as the agency of change in international society. War, except in self-defence, has lost its legitimacy, so terrorism takes over its job.

The implication of this kind of observation is that terrorism, far from being uniformly a challenge to international order, might be in some sense a constituent of it. And Adam Roberts, in his chapter, considered the possibility that order might be maintained, at least in the short run, by frightening people into submission to a tyrannical regime. But we may doubt whether an order of this kind would be worth defending against a terrorist challenge. Taking the broader conception of order with which we began this book, the first item in it was the idea that it is the violent interruption of the business of everyday life that we object to when we speak of a terrorist challenge to international order. The statistics presented by Paul Wilkinson are disturbing, especially the increasing lethality of terrorist attacks. But the sheer brute numbers are not moving when compared, for example, with the 20,000 killed annually in the United States as a result of 'ordinary crime'.[2] It is the cold-bloodedly deliberate taking of innocent life that is the offence to order given by terrorism. But we may doubt whether this is a challenge to *international* order in the sense either of the security of the states-system as a whole or of its individual constituents.

This international order might be taken to be under threat if the legitimacy of the state, as the holder of the monopoly on violence within its frontiers, was under widespread challenge by terrorist groups. But to assert that this was happening would be to see an anarchist in every terrorist. The PLO, the IRA, ETA, the South Moluccans, and so on, want a *place* in the states-system, not to bring it down. And while there are groups, as Paul Wilkinson reminded us, such as the German Red Army Faction, and the French Action Directe, whose objectives are not straightforwardly patriotic, it would be hard to establish that they had even begun to succeed in eroding the legitimacy of the states or the system in which they operate.

What then of *state* terrorism, the kind which does seem directly to confront the institutions of international society on which the state terrorists themselves ordinarily survive? The state which sponsors the kidnapping or murder of the diplomats of another state, or which pursues its own nationals in vendettas carried on in third states, or which supports a terrorist faction in a civil war in another state, makes a direct attack on fundamental principles of international order (the immunity of diplomats; the principle of state sovereignty; and the principle of non-intervention). By doing so it might also weaken the whole fabric of international order by reducing the incentive for reciprocal restraint by others. Hence the concern of international society about this question, and the responses to it which Adam Roberts discussed in his chapter. There are, however, two factors which reduce the impact of this challenge. The first is that not all states, not even a substantial minority of states, are engaged in state terrorism. Philip Windsor can deal with it as a maverick activity (though his conclusion is that state terrorists are not necessarily mavericks, and mavericks not necessarily terrorists). The second is, as Lawrence Freedman observes in his chapter, that states when they meddle in terrorist activity prefer to do it covertly so that they are not seen to be directly confronting the rules of the game—which may be taken to reflect some respect for norms of international behaviour.

Our final item of order concerned the question of terror-international, and of a general challenge to the international order. Has terrorism become, as Philip Windsor wonders, an 'autonomous activity', not linked to its sources in any particular political context but merely 'terrorism for terrorism's sake'? Should it be treated, as Adam Roberts asks, as a 'global phenomenon'—not as the outgrowth of this or that society or the result of particular injustices?

In the nature of things, the existence of such a 'global phenomenon' is hard to establish, since participants in it are unlikely to announce themselves as such, and the interpretation of their activity depends as much on the political predispositions of the interpreter as on the stream of data coming from events in the 'real world'. But, in the absence of a global polity competent to meet its demands, the existence of a global tribe of nomadic terrorists, united only by their will to frighten the rest of us, seems inherently implausible. Whereas the existence of several groups, with less than global aspirations, some of which cooperate in some degree on matters of common interest, seems a reasonable hypothesis.[3] The challenge they together present to international order may be significant but not cataclysmic.

For this reason, we might share the doubts of the sceptics about the challenge of 'low-intensity warfare'. It conjures up a vision of a single enemy in a world which, in fact, is more complex, and it leaves some Europeans more concerned about the judgment of their friends than about the intentions of their enemies. Nevertheless, the methods of the terrorist do threaten the international order in a way that cannot simply be dismissed by referring to the small numbers of incidents, or to the robustness of the states-system. Adam Roberts showed, in his chapter, how terrorists might hollow out the state, leaving a mere shell to confront the international system—as in the case of Lebanon. He also dealt with the difficulties which terrorists raise in a normative system which depends on a clear distinction between the domestic and the international, self-defence and aggression, the regime of peace and that of war. Terrorists are difficult to confine to one or other in these pairs of opposites, and in this lies the problem for the response to terrorism.

We may consider our conclusions on the response to terrorism in four aspects: prevention, the immediate reaction, the reaction to the host-state, and the long-term response. On the prevention of terrorism through deterrence and penalties, Paul Wilkinson calls for more intensive international cooperation than currently exists, though he stresses that we are talking about the reduction, not elimination, of terrorism. On the immediate reaction, when confronted by the demand of terrorists who have taken hostages, three broad responsive patterns have been suggested:[4] *flexible response*, in which negotiations are entered into immediately; *safe release*, in which the chief concern is for the safety of the hostages, and where the 'Bangkok solution' (release of hostages plus safe passage for the terrorists) might be the optimum one; and *strict no-concessions*, in which the chief concern is said to be the discouragement of future acts of terrorism by not allowing this one to bear any fruit.

The question of dealing with the state that plays host to terrorists, or itself sponsors terrorism, is more difficult. Our authors, notably Adam Roberts and Lawrence Freedman, have dealt with the difficulties that attach to the 'police plus non-violent sanctions' approach and the military approach to the means by which the struggle against terrorism should be conducted. In either case, the control over the outcome is limited. And both responses face the problem of spreading and aggravating the disease that they nominally aim to cure. This aim may of course *be* purely nominal. Richard Falk has argued that there is little evidence that any of the inner circle of the Reagan administration which took the decision to bomb Libya believed that it would abate terrorist activity.[5] And he shows that the Munich analogy, pressed into service again, this time as a mainstream American criticism of the European response to the terrorist threat, is crucially flawed. The logic of the Munich analogy is strike now in order to avoid a heavier price if you leave it till later. Whereas, in the case of the Libyan raids, the logic was strike now even though it might encourage further terrorism.[6] And Lawrence Freedman above took the argument a step further. The greatest problem with such a counterterrorist strategy, he suggested, was when it became necessary to return to the fray. The target is alerted, the impact less great, and any pretence that counterterrorism might reduce terrorism exposed.

Moreover, it is difficult to know where to stop when targeting countries that aid terrorists or employ their tactics themselves. Brian Jenkins runs up a list of twenty such states, and maintains that it could easily be doubled[7] (although there is room for a great deal of argument here about what 'aiding terrorism' is, and who sponsors it). A great power taking on the responsibility of policing such a system would be dangerously exposed to the charge that its action was undermining what fragile order had been achieved in international relations rather than buttressing it. The plausible defence of the order-keeper—that what it was doing might not stop terrorism, but would increase the costs of taking part in it—becomes a vigilante argument rather than a police one. In this regard, Adam Roberts, in the light of the International Court of Justice's judgment in the Nicaragua case, is sceptical of the authority of great powers, and is more inclined to look for measures of international cooperation that can command a wide consensus.

There were finally the political dilemmas dealt with by Christopher Hill in the longer perspective and in Paul Wilkinson's account of American policy. Wilkinson documents the increasing salience of terrorism for policy-makers and public opinion in the US. This salience is unlikely to decrease, and indeed may be accentuated by American frustration at the less assertive European response. In the relations among the Western powers, Hill concluded, terrorism did not of itself cause a serious breach—though there were important differences of mood and style between the reaction of the United States and that of the bulk of the West European powers. In particular, he depicted a difference between an American willingness to depend on the rationality of using force as a counter and deterrent to terrorist force, and a European tendency to prefer diplomacy and the search for political solutions. But, as Hill goes on to argue, this is as much a result of the structure of the system, and of the roles of the various actors within it, as it is the result of any reasoned disquisition on the nature of the terrorist threat to international order. Because of this structural constraint, and because of divisions within movements that have used terrorism, we should not expect (as Windsor points out) a 'reasonable' response to the 'just claims' of terrorists to do away with the problem of terrorism—even though there may be such just claims.

There is a sense in which the 'terrorist menace' fits into a pattern of thought that has been constructed over centuries by those who see themselves as the guardians of order in international relations. Before it, there was the Soviet threat, and the communist challenge, and before them the danger of liberal nationalism, and before that the menace of Jacobinism keeping up a spirit of insurrection against all governments. It is this pattern of thought that the critics of the United States have seized on in expressing their attitude to the Reagan administration's policy towards terrorism in general, and the raids on Libya in particular.[8] But, just as the menace of 'low-intensity warfare' is hard to accept as an undifferentiated threat to the position of the West in the world, so the radicals' criticism of 'terrorism' as a put-up job to disguise American hegemony does violence to a reality that is more complex. In this regard, we should not take at face value the rhetoric either of those, speaking for Third World countries, who have been concerned to depict the United States as the linchpin of a structure of dependence which might rely on terrorism for its maintenance, or of those in the West who take the terrorism of non-Western groups to be the greatest threat to the civilization that has been nurtured by the West.

It is the more complex reality between these positions that we have sought to catch a glimpse of, while trying to assess the implications for order among states of the methods of the terrorist. And we recognize, too, that what happens in the future in Libya, for example, will condition our judgment of the implications of violent 'counterterrorism'. Whatever that future, the implications of transnational terrorism for the maintenance of order are neither negligible, nor are they overwhelming. If they were either, the task for foreign policy would be easier.

Notes

1. Michael Walzer, *Just and Unjust Wars* (London, Allen Lane, 1977), p. 197.
2. See B.M. Jenkins, 'Combatting Terrorism: Some Policy Implications', Rand Paper P-666 (Rand Corporation, Santa Monica, CA, August 1981), p. 7.
3. Brian Jenkins has discussed the 'possible emergence' of multinational freelance terrorist groups. See Jenkins, 'Testimony Before the Senate Governmental Affairs Committee Regarding Senate Bill Against Terrorism', Rand Paper No. P-6596 (Rand Corporation, Santa Monica, CA, February 1981), p. 3. It is more reasonable to suppose that they will be hired by a local than a global tribe.
4. This useful division comes from Gail Bass, *et al.*, *Options for US Policy on Terrorism*, Rand Publication Series, Report No. R-2764-RC (Rand Corporation, Santa Monica, CA, July 1981), pp. 4–5.
5. Richard Falk, 'Rethinking counter-terrorism', in Mary Kaldor and Paul Anderson (eds.), *Mad Dogs* (London, Pluto, 1986), p. 129.
6. In this respect, Senator Mark Hatfield's attitude is characteristic. He is quoted as saying the Libyan raid was bad policy but 'It feels good.' *Middle East Economic Digest*, 19 April 1986, p. 7.
7. Jenkins, 'Combatting Terrorism', pp. 3–4.
8. See especially E.P. Thompson, 'Letter to Americans', in Kaldor and Anderson, *Mad Dogs*.

Statistical appendix to Chapter 4

Table 4.1 A comparison between ITERATE,* CIA and Rand Corporation estimates of incidents of international terrorism and deaths in international terrorist incidents for the years 1968–77

Year	Number of incidents per year			Number of deaths per year		
	ITERATE	CIA	RAND	ITERATE	CIA	RAND
1968	123	111	35	34	34	21
1969	179	166	51	26	29	7
1970	344	282	101	125	110	74
1971	301	216	52	36	36	7
1972	480	269	84	153	145	130
1973	340	275	163	117	124	92
1974	425	382	153	328	315	247
1975	342	297	89	240	240	92
1976	455	413	151	409	402	200
1977	340	279	143	277	235	145
Totals	3,329	2,690	1,022	1,745	1,670	1,015

*ITERATE—International Terrorism: Attributes of Terrorist Events computer system.
Sources: Edward F. Mickolus, Transnational Terrorism: A Chronology of Events, 1968–79 (London, Aldwych Press, 1980)—ITERATE.
Central Intelligence Agency, International Terrorism in 1979 (Washington, DC, April 1980), pp. xiii–xxx—CIA.
B. M. Jenkins, 'International Terrorism: trends and potentialities', Journal of International Affairs, vol. 32 (1978), no. 1, pp. 114–23—RAND.

Table 4.2 Geographic distribution of international terrorist incidents, 1968–79

Location	1968	1969	1970	1971	1972	1973	1974	1975	1976	1977	1978	1979	Total*
North America	35	7	23	24	18	18	38	51	37	23	19	25	318(9.5)
Latin America	41	71	113	70	49	80	124	48	105	46	61	53	861(25.8)
Western Europe	16	31	58	38	112	141	151	109	179	129	166	137	1,267(38.0)
USSR/Eastern Europe	0	1	0	2	1	0	1	2	0	2	3	3	15(0.4)
Sub-Saharan Africa	0	7	8	4	4	4	9	18	16	20	24	10	124(3.7)
Middle East & N. Africa	18	32	60	52	35	21	47	56	62	48	61	39	531(15.9)
Asia	1	12	19	24	43	10	11	13	14	8	16	26	197(5.9)
Oceania	0	5	1	2	3	1	1	0	0	3	3	0	19(0.6)
Transregional	0	0	0	0	4	0	0	0	0	0	0	0	4(0.1)
Total	111	166	282	216	269	275	382	297	413	279	353	293	3,336

*Figures in parentheses are percentages of the total accounted for by each region. (The total for North America appears in the original as 11.4 and has been corrected.)
Source: US National Assessment Center, International Terrorism in 1979 (Washington, DC, 1980).

Table 4.3 International terrorist attacks on US citizens or property, 1968–79, by category of target

Target	1968	1969	1970	1971	1972	1973	1974	1975	1976	1977	1978	1979	Total*
Diplomatic officials or property	12	17	52	51	22	19	12	12	12	21	22	21	273(20.3)
Military officials or property	4	2	38	36	11	12	12	9	33	10	30	7	204(15.1)
Other government officials or property	26	32	57	21	20	10	16	14	2	7	2	10	217(16.1)
Business facilities or executives	6	35	24	40	44	51	86	42	52	33	47	27	487(36.2)
Private citizens	3	7	17	5	12	10	13	27	26	13	21	12	166(12.3)
Total	51	93	188	153	109	102	139	104	125	84	122	77	1,347

*Figures in parentheses are percentages of the total accounted for by each category of target.
Source: US National Assessment Center, *International Terrorism in 1979* (Washington, DC, 1980).

Table 4.4 International terrorist incidents against US citizens and property, 1980–5

Incident	1980	1981	1982	1983	1984	1985	Total
Total	163	159	208	199	131	177	1,037
Armed attack	33	27	17	25	19	17	138
Armed occupation and barricade	4	—	2	6	—	—	12
Arson	23	25	58	34	9	29	178
Assault, intimidation, extortion	—	—	—	—	3	4	7
Bombing	62	71	109	93	70	95	500
Hostage-taking and barricade	4	1	1	2	3	—	11
Kidnapping	10	10	8	9	14	18	69
Skyjacking	1	9	1	1	6	4	22
Other	26	16	12	29	7	10	100

Source: US Department of State, Patterns of Global Terrorism, 1984 (Washington, DC, 1985).

Figure 4.1 Geographic distribution of international terrorist incidents, 1984 (%)

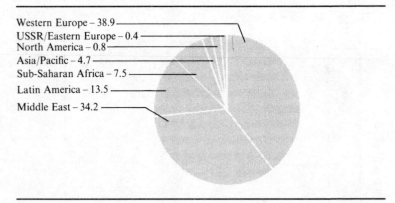

Western Europe – 38.9
USSR/Eastern Europe – 0.4
North America – 0.8
Asia/Pacific – 4.7
Sub-Saharan Africa – 7.5
Latin America – 13.5
Middle East – 34.2

Source: US Department of State, *Patterns of Global Terrorism, 1984* (Washington, DC, 1985).